BEST *of* AUSTRALIAN POEMS 2023

ACKNOWLEDGEMENT OF COUNTRY

Australian Poetry is based
in Naarm, Melbourne, working
in offices and remotely on both
Wurundjeri Woi Wurrung and
Boon Wurrung lands.
We acknowledge their Elders,
past and present. As a national
poetry body, we also acknowledge
that we work across many lands and
communities, and we extend our
deep respect to all First Peoples, not
just in Australia, but across the globe,
including poets and audiences, and
their enduring connection
to Country.

Best of Australian Poems
SERIES PUBLISHER
Australian Poetry

BEST *of* AUSTRALIAN POEMS 2023

GUEST EDITORS

GIG RYAN

&

PANDA WONG

Australian Poetry

First published 2023 by
Australian Poetry
www.australianpoetry.com

National Library of Australia
Cataloguing-in-Publication data:

Best of australian poems 2023
ISBN: 978-0-9923189-4-9

Series Publisher: Australian Poetry
AP Managing Editor: Adalya Nash Hussein
AP Communications and Editorial Associate: Jennifer Nguyen
AP Publisher: Jacinta Le Plastrier
Founding Designer & Cover Designer: Sophie Gaur
Designer & Typesetter: Chris Edwards
Printer: Lightning Source

Publisher's Note:
AP would like to deeply thank all the publishers, platforms and other organisations that support the flourishing and publishing of Australian poetry. While some of these *BoAP 2023* poems were selected in open call-out, many were previously published by these great forces. It is AP's policy as Publisher to also keep 'arm's length' in the selection of poems by our guest editors, where we have different guest editors across our numerous, annual publications. Regarding *BoAP 2023*, we do work to ensure that poems fall within the set, strict timeframe. AP's house style is to accept a poet's choice of titling capitalisation, choice of punctuation and spelling styles, so across the book there is a natural variation allowed. Finally a number of patrons have contributed funds to this particular project. To these, and our core funders and project partners, profound thanks. This project has been assisted by the Australian Government through Creative Australia (formerly known as the Australia Council), its arts funding and advisory body. This volume's launch has been funded by the Copyright Agency Cultural Fund.

Australian Government
Creative Australia
CREATIVE VICTORIA
United Nations Educational, Scientific and Cultural Organization
Melbourne City of Literature
The Wheeler Centre Books Writing Ideas
COPYRIGHT AGENCY CULTURAL FUND

Foreword

We acknowledge that editing, producing and publishing *Best of Australian Poems 2023* took place on the traditional lands of the Boon Wurrung and Wurundjeri Woi Wurrung First Nations peoples. The poems included in this anthology come from a range of sovereign First Nations lands. We note that poetry is never separate from the lands, waters and skies it is created in, and pay our respects to the long, enduring histories of poetry and storytelling. Sovereignty has never been ceded. It always was, and always will be Aboriginal land.

Best of Australian Poems 2023 is the third in a series of annual anthologies from national poetry organisation Australian Poetry, aiming to capture a poetic snapshot of the year (in this case, work written or published between 1 July 2022–1 August 2023). 'Best' is a strange and loaded term, but in editing *Best of Australian Poems 2023*, we interpreted it as the best representation of what is happening in Australian poetry at this specific moment in time—what poets were feeling, thinking, and imagining across many different forms, mediums and lexicons. Aside from its archival purposes, *Best of Australian Poems 2023* will be a space of discovery, where readers can encounter new poets.

Continuing in the rhythms of the 2021 and 2022 anthologies—which were respectively guest-edited by Ellen van Neerven and Toby Fitch, and Jeanine Leane and Judith Beveridge—we have chosen 100 of Australia's most original, interesting and vital poems, work that represents the range and multiplicity of Australian poetry. We thank our predecessors for their careful reading and sourcing, which set a standard we were determined to uphold in our co-editorship.

More poets than ever before sent work to our callout, with submissions comprising half of this anthology, emphasising how open calls can bring forward strong work outside of our immediate familiarity. In addition to reading submissions, we read chapbooks, collections, journals (online and print), newspapers and magazines. With the knowledge that poetry is often an exploration of form, we listened to poetry recordings and soundscapes, watched readings and performances, and delved into exhibitions and artistic projects that spanned poetry. We were also committed to the inclusion of digitally specific poetry and had many conversations on how to best represent this on the printed page. This form speaks to the multi-dimensional and borderless ways in which we process and share information at this time, and we felt it was important to include it as a rapidly emerging (and exciting!) part of Australian poetry. With the recent death of John Tranter, it has been interesting to look back on his meticulously edited and comprehensive *jacket* (one of the first online literary journals when it appeared in 1997), to consider how many more online journals have come about since and how many are featured in this collection.

Reading the thousands of poems was a huge task, spanning a variety of liminal spaces within and around the seams of our daily lives. This way of reading brings to mind what poet and academic Anne Boyer wrote, '… how a person should read is how a person must read, which is at least in duplicate, both always in this world and looking for another.' When reading in the co-editorship model, we not only looked for poems that spoke to each other of place, peerage and time—but also to each other as co-editors to shape and challenge our own poetic tastes and preferences. Bringing together our different viewpoints and practices was critical in this process.

Our many discussions over email and Zoom allowed us to explore and learn from our different poetic ideas, preferences and specific knowledges. It has been an interesting experience to collaborate, to find many of our choices were the same, to elaborate on the quality of each poem, to sometimes disagree but often easily reach consensus.

As editors, we have been aesthetically discriminating but we have also hoped to represent many of the current variations in styles. Some poems entertain an absurdist humour often finishing with a mordant flourish, others follow their own constraints or algorithms; occasionally there is adherence to more formal verse. This anthology includes narrative poems, prose poems, lyric and anti-lyric poems; list poems; archival poetry; spoken word or slam poetry, sound poetry; concrete poems; poems written for music; poems of resistance; ecopoetry; poems making use of other languages, including First Nations languages; digital poetry; visual poetry—ekphrastic poetry, surrealist, collage and conceptual poems; collaborative poems; long poems, short poems; prize-winning poems, previously unpublished poems; love poems; elegies; epistolary poems; ars poetica and more.

Not only is this anthology diverse in form, but it spans a large number of dreams, concerns, fears, hopes, anxieties and ideas—we have poems reflecting on domesticity; poems that question or revise historical events; poems in opposition to colonialism, racism, government policy, the patriarchy, capitalism and other oppressive systems; poems that are a call to action; poems that explore gender, the body, the abject, states of being; poems that gesture towards the divine, spirituality, mythology and the sublime; poems centred on introspection, and poems that look outward to the Anthropocene world we inhabit; poems about our relationships with people, plants and animals; poems about ecological disaster and capitalist crisis; but also poems that retain optimism, that look to the future imagining new realms and possibilities. Many poems refer to other arts: to painters Gerhard Richter, Sidney Nolan, Mirka Mora; to writers Kathy Acker, Bernadette Meyer, Dorothy Porter, and many refer to music.

We have chosen poets from many different cultural backgrounds, ages, genders and from across the country, creating as broad a cross-section of Australian poetry as we could, given the constraints of a printed anthology. Many of Australia's most accomplished poets are published alongside new and emerging voices, reflecting Australian poetry's constant growth and evolution.

There were certainly many more poems that we could have added if space had allowed—both that we read, and that we couldn't. With the breadth and scale of the task at hand, it was impossible for us to read every single poem written and published within the timeframe. Aside from our physical limitations, there are limitations to the printed page, and it is impossible to represent all the different forms of poetry that exist—such as the oral and temporal poetry of protests, community gatherings, and the home. We echo previous co-editors in recognising that these works hold deep value outside of the printed page and institutions, and the need for them to be recognised and platformed outside of traditional publishing.

This past year has also seen the deaths of some of Australia's most recognised poets, including Catherine Vidler (1973–2023),

Andrew Rutherford (1968–2022), Alison Flett (1965–2023), Robert Adamson (1943–2022), John Tranter (1943–2023). It is impossible to name all who have passed, including emerging or marginalised voices whose work we may not even know, but we hope to honour their immense contributions to poetry, publishing, editing, criticism and their communities.

This anthology would not be possible without the work of many. We are thankful for the input and efficiency of Adalya Nash Hussein who has acted as Managing Editor, as well as to the other Australian Poetry staff—publisher Jacinta Le Plastrier, designers Sophie Gaur and Chris Edwards, and on marketing and communications, Jennifer Nguyen—for the devoted support, trust and the countless hours of work they have dedicated to this anthology. Many thanks also to the Wheeler Centre for their ongoing partnership with Australian Poetry, and for generously hosting the *Best of Australian Poems 2023* launch, which will take place in early 2024.

We thank all the publications and organisations that supported and published many of the poems here, the full list of which can be found in the acknowledgements. We also thank those whose work and support have contributed to this fertile and ever-changing poetic landscape, including this series's predecessor, Black Inc.'s *The Best Australian Poems* (2003–2017).

Finally, we thank all poets who produced work this year, and who submitted to the open callout. We were grateful to intensively read such a wide variety of writing and to expand our knowledge of contemporary Australian poetry in the process.

When considering the order of poems, we have followed the model used thus far, placing poems by title in alphabetical order, and prioritising the poem itself. We hope that you, our readers, will be provoked, intrigued and entertained by the poems within this anthology.

—*Gig Ryan & Panda Wong*

Contents

POEMS

After writing a book on female autism, I decide to bury it

Esther Ottaway |

Go on with that public Esther, curated pretense:
to be and not to be, that is Australian.

What good are these chalk traces around spent victims?
Why lift the sheet on myself, fatigued, confounded?

I know what I'd be next: that bleating woman,
the blaring car alarm that barely registers.

Truth-pregnant, I laboured. Her name is Repercussions.
My fear: that this child kicks, draws breath to cry.

After reading her poem, I remember the diagnosis they give me | *Andy Jackson*

Monstrous, so I speak well, as distraction or defense,
but my achilles heel is that I'm mammalian.

What tweezers might extract these brutal dictums?
Isn't this reticence, this fear, well-founded?

Ashamed and proud to have failed as a man,
my flesh holds these undissolveable slurs.

Hunch-drunk, I stagger, assailed by concussions.
No point getting up, this stigma says. In these lines, I try.

as we are | *ALISON J BARTON*

after Jeanine Leane's 'As We Are: A Call Across The Islands'

the colonial state curates a fiction

of brutal modernity

insistent settlers

entrap

place-time

is

rich

with vast storying

an act of *being*
a gesture

that

bonds

the mythscape alive and breathing

storytellers

break

grow

plait

Note: This is a found poem inspired by the essay 'As We Are: A Call Across The Islands', written by Jeanine Leane, published in *Sydney Review of Books*, 29 November 2021, which reviews the book *Shapes of Native Nonfiction: Collected Essays by Contemporary Writers*, by Elissa Washuta and Teresa Warburton (editors). The poet has altered some terms from how they appeared in the original essay.

In Brazil, so I read, the Doberman pinscher is celebrated,
and aestheticised, through the use of bandages. Twins—in reality,
survivors of larger litters—often bark together. When on a stage
they're probably looking for someone. A poetry of the self

Requires a lot of doubling, beautifying, or other change, if it is
to remain interesting. In Brazil, or so I read, there is more interest
in futurism than in the Vatican. But this is not news. Poetry is not dated
by its news content. I dated someone once: you guessed it, they were

Brazilian, and named Thoreau, after the great glider pilot. His smile
was like the sky or an eel. The artist's throat peels, as they stand
among the trees. They cannot be heard clearly, through their mask.
Proximity interests me, however, as does attachment. To live as several

Identities, or none, is different to dying, that is, how we die:
with the dot hovering, like a drop of blood, above the 'i'. What is going
to happen? The dogs' black and tan noses lift from their jaws to bark.
What are they barking at? Fame? Ignominy? The audience's silence?

Biladurang untranslated | JEANINE LEANE

You stop me in my tracks when I
see you in the Grand Gallery of Evolution
at the Musee d'histoire naturelle
on Rue Geoffroy Saint-Hilaire – a mythical
place so the citation says where modernity meets history
and science tells the story of great adventure.

I trace you
from top to toe and back again
with my eyes among 7000 species collected
and displayed. *Ornithorhynchus anatinus* –
phylum: Chordata; class: Mammalia; order:
Monotremata. Australian platypus.

On a river a million miles away
where I walked as a child you are biladurang.
My Gunhinurrung stooped with stick,
black hair turned to ash, still walking the river
told me your name. From Mundarlo Bridge
to the Nangus floodplain we'd watch you arch
and dive your rippled story deep into the dark water.

Derrida said
every text remains in mourning until it is translated.
I wander through these display cabinets of
butterflies and moths pinned to boards, reptiles
marinating in jars of ethanol, birds, and animals
stuffed, splayed out and labelled in Latin
behind glass and wonder.

Are you not already known biladurung,
on Country that birthed you – shaped you
through lands and waters. Named you through story.
On the other side of this translation
a river somewhere will remember you –
or a mountain, a ridge, a plain, a gully or a creek
will know you by your name.

Biladurung it's your capture you mourn behind
those glass eyes that stare out at me.
When I speak your name out loud – biladurung
I give it back to you from the river where I
first heard it – the river that still remembers you
free and untranslated.

Note: 'every text remains in mourning until it is translated' has also been attributed to Derrida's Arabic translator, Kadhim Jihad Hassan. The quote comes to us in English from writer and translator Sinan Antoon's lecture 'Translation and the Work of Mourning'.

Blade of Grass, Meadow of Knives | DAN HOGAN

Summer equals cicadascream plus other superimpositions
hung in the air like an idea of bunting but never the worsted
wool. I'm no mathematician but who is? Nobody in this poor
excuse for a nondescript prism hurtling birthdaytowardbirthday
toward your tenth coffee is free. A popout cake is a large prop
designed to resemble a cake in which a person emerges to the
surprise of outsiders. Innovation and jobs and growth have seen
a little seat inside. When the alarm went off this morning I wasn't
yet the genealogy of an image but who is? Who? Everybody inside
a popout cake has two wolves inside them. Both are domesticated.
One is a Chihuahua/Pomeranian cross. The other is red. Anyway,
there is no gimmick like home. I once knew a Pomeranian who,
despite the limits of their form, taught me 'bagel' is short for
'baby angel'. I digress. But also: when in Rome? When in
Rome stuff a pie full of doves and frogs and have them burst forth
for your guests. This is all to say grief is a detour. (When in
Rome!) I desire for this loss to manifest as something (anything)
handsome in writing but all I've got is this fixation on popout
cakes and the loudest cicadas are the ones who stayed
in the ground the longest. But don't take my word for it. Ear
to the ground until the lawn's urge has cut through to the other
side. Blade of grass? Meadow of knives! Find a verandah and wait.
See what I'm saying? When in the yard ask yourself: what fangs
out of the bracken with a head full of garden? The answer and
everything on this page is

Blue | D. PEREZ-MCVIE

I wonder what you see in me.
A bluish scar, blue giving way to
Blue, a warm unnecessary feeling
Sat on or saturated by, against an
Improbably clear and permissive

Light. A fold, of course, always
Folds with me, folds and folds.
An open sense of dwelling, no
Significant reasons for not trying.
The way disclosure

Predicates and predates
Sand. An incursion of feeling
Along all lines, upward along
The spine. Upward from my
Heartspace. A space, a space

Not yet dominated by

Your

Camp indigo will.

I'm anxious about

And elated by

Not understanding

The raw essence of whatever's

Going on.

Blue belted

Hazchem distinctions. I'm angrier
When I'm free of your gaze.
You know it ends in sweetness.
An impatient balloon structure
Suited to fabulations. A suite

For uncouth blue foraging.
A star witnessing genuflection.
Ready to be debased again.
It's pretty cool actually. A
Gloved resistance to facts and

Crime statistics. Crying is still
The best resource I have. A
Gloved resistance, an extra large
Disposable powdered latex guy
Between folds of fake fleece.

A continuation of
Childhood's vibes.
My heart flushing, and
A tear rolling back into
My pewter eye.

Bluebottles | JUDITH BEVERIDGE

So many swimmers ran out of the sea, branded with welts
or wearing scarlet copies of the tentacles of a swarm of bluebottles.
They limped, yelled, rubbed sand, or poured water on the stingers,
and some, unsure of the correct first aid, applied ice cream,

even sunscreen, anything at hand: soft drink, hot coffee—
and some already sunburned, felt the stingers like a further
blowtorch, a raw franking, a due payment of blisters.
On the sand the bluebottles looked like air-filled dumplings,

tight balloons of nothing, soap bubbles on top of small bags
of laundry bluing. Kids with sticks burst the bulbous floats
or slapped them with their thongs, making the sound of corks
fired from popguns. Some lifted the tentacles high then flung

them away to make strange patterns on the sand. I've never
held to divine supplication or sympathetic magic, never worn
charms or lucky pieces, but that day I whispered a prayer
that no tentacles clothe me in pitiless scarlet, that no barbs

pierce my body with the lightning-quick, punching power
of tattoo needles, that I don't run out of the sea with my skin
turning into flocked wallpaper, my arms bearing a mock-up
of my veins, my legs a sea-creature's long hieroglyphics for pain.

Boarding House | π.o.

Bugs, mosquitoes, fleas,
and flies,... down the stairs anybody's...
everyone's / Anyone's / Nobody's.
It's not in the Landlord's wine, to make
a boarding-house *Welcoming*;
The arsehole who said, that the *soup*
they got, could have tasted better if *all* the dishes
had been washed in it first, didn't get
that soup in a boarding house. You have to remember
to always look behind the wardrobe to see
where all the cockroaches live; how
the other ½ live. It's the lack of contact
with other people, that makes people feel lonely.
I remember walking up a lane 2 in the morning
an' this arsehole offering to let me sleep
at his place. — Lots of horrible shit! —
Isolation is a room you can't get out of.
People look at a picture of you, and
think you're Okay. I tried to commit
suicide ///// 5 times! The people across the street
told the Landlord everything in the back-
ground was stolen. All my family
call me an *Idiot.* (You *feed-off* that) (and
your own *negativity*). Nobody understands how
anyone can say they "can't" eat (living
in accommodation with only $2 left
for a pie). When i couldn't relate (like when
i took sleeping tablets) i drank. *Who* i am is *How* i am!
Hand in hand with tears, and sad.
You're holding on, and (not just family)
are telling you, the most important thing to do
is to "just let go". Lots of people are dead inside.

I walked away with a Tv once. (Don't know
what triggered that). (Owed a lot of money
i guess). (All over the place). (Rent up
the shit). (Months of it). An Alcoholic needs
help to get up the ///// steps… to place
the key in the right space. (They can't find
their own feet). A performer is suppose
to make an audience *laugh* every 7 secs; sitting with
anxiety, and *effecting* a broken voice;
"I Don't Live Here Anymore!!!".
You just have to "Get on with it (i
guess)". If they call in a control freak
you're *dead meat!* — "Get a proper job!" (playing
at a shitty little warehouse gig). (Stealing music
to liven up the gig). (Being pushed to
breaking point. By some arsehole) (in
the crowd). "Everyone else" *isn't* a good
start to a sentence. Then… a *full*
drum-kit [kick] ✓ and a *calculated*
stumble, ends it all. [Repeat]. And
the session ends, to *disinterested*

/ // / applause.

Bose-Einstein Condensate

how we look at superfluidity and superconductivity

| *ALICIA SOMETIMES*
WITH SOUND BY ANDREA RASSELL

states of matter

within a shiver
of absolute zero

atoms slow
drawn-out
languid

so cold
they band

together

every particle
at once
everywhere

wave packets
swaying

elongating
embellishing

bosons

losing identity
flow forming

(listen

(the closer we are
(we crumble into

(black pools
(we become one
(scattering into

(time-thin
(mantles cooling

(on the surface

(we pulverise
(into embers
(teaspoonful

(by teaspoonful
(you are fibres

(sleepless
(we are soaring

(into the thick

(of things
(listen

overlapping	(to the numbing
decoherence	(dark
where one ends	(learn from
another begins	(this wave-function
within a quake	(cold matters
we are	(at rest

Scan QR code to listen to the sound component of this poem, created by Andrea Rassell, on *Baby Teeth Journal*'s website.

Bourne Again | EVA BIRCH

sad Alicia Vikander had to give up

her erotic life in Jason Bourne

except for the little trackers

slipped into her pockets

he leaves her a phone or a camera

or something with a video of her

betraying him

Bourne

always stealing and leaving phones

like hand grenades

wait, my phone is blowing up

wait, it's just a text from you about the lecture

I was kinda like Alicia in the library

when Matt came in with the batteries

for the field recorder

and I slipped them into the

pocket of my suit jacket

like oh yeahhhh

being a poet is kinda like being in the CIA

killing everything with phone—

nemes

at your park party

you said Joan Didion wasn't safe

because of her style and it made me sad because

the last time you said something wasn't safe

was when I spilt boiling water on my vagina

and you helped me back

into the world

young guy with mother flow

like the poem with the

Babadook and freezing eggs

that's what I wanna do this year
by the way
get those little fuckers

pure pearls of dusk

low key future saints

I said what are we doing? at the third location
what do you mean? you said in a really angry voice
like that was the big question you
were trying to get at with
the whole party thing

I regret taking the sunglasses from the uber
my first feeling about them
was correct
they had evil energy

the sunglasses are like what some
evil assassin would wear in Bourne

or Joan Didion when she was

younger but still

unsafe

it's ok to larp as an evil assassin

batteries in my jacket

like I'm Vincent Cassel

chasing Matt Damon in an Audi

cars falling either side of us

like a machine harvesting radishes

like when we were driving, wasted

on the tram tracks and you were

impressed with my reflexes

it was really Bourne when

you went to New York

I gotta say

it's the main reason

I'm not giving up on this poem

when you were over there so urgently

I was back at the park

pulling teaspoons out

of my backpack

Bourne mode

teaspoons are holy, ice cream is holy,

Royal Park is holy, obviously,

the vagina is holy

because it's a HOLE

but also when something's going in it

like a cock and there's a lot of

pressure but it's ok

I can handle it

and it's so weird and nice

and I come and

you come

before we did it I imagined it

as something so big, something

that went beyond me, through the park

and the trees and the sky

I could smell spring

coming

it was really Bourne when I gave the lecture too

with you but also without you

adidas and cotton and the

kind of control that's easy and sexy

in a safe way, like how you go full speed

and I can't keep up but maybe

I kinda can

when you force me to be

Bourne again

Alicia, holding down the fort at the office with

the big screens, while Matt moves

the phones around into different pockets

and stuff, it's all moving too fast and

you can't work out why he's started tracking

her, doesn't he trust her?

and the movie in general moves too fast

but that's because everything *does* move

too fast now so maybe that's what makes

it a good film for breaking into

and then breaking out of

IDEOLOGY

POETRY

the Great Media of Our Age

also does this

when I'm riding my bike along the city trail

and I see a boat that says BLACK-OPS

that's Bourne-poetry

when I post it on Instagram

that's a mood board for my

Bourne poem

a party *always* has a mood

this poem is a party

and the mood is POETRY

and more specifically

BOURNE-POETRY

it was drinking matcha that allowed me to

enter Bourne mode

and sex

sex is Bourne

because in Jason Bourne, the film

there's no sex

it's so frustrating and erotic

like

just do it

Mel*bourne,* obviously very Bourne

born

again and again

in Melbourne

giving each other batteries for energy

harvesting phonemes like little radishes

writing the dirt and the veggies

back into the movies

like Bourne

like

yeah

Camperdown Grief Junk | YEENA KIRKBRIGHT

In wombhole I meet feathered oracle, cross-legged and knowin'
tells me I know nothin' of time. "Listen 'ere Sis, don't waste it
it's slippin' by while yous humans fuck everythin' up"
Languorin' now by springtime wound
swimmin' where the light enters, warns me
when sun lays horizontal on graves dusk heavy
her coeval nebula will then be callin' home.

Before flight takes her, sends me down to Aunty
Wandaiyalle by South Wall
where we could be ibis stalkin'
through misty antediluvian
newspaper headlines yellin'
but nobody listenin'
Women Of So-called 'Nation' Most Unsafe In Own Homes 2022
This 'er now time where violent men be fresh
not fettered by polite free-market-gentlemanry
still as if only yesterday 'im did not sin
as if gods had not forsaken all
and gifted 'im incentives to be satan
incentives to be takin
'em women and fashionin' wives of 'em
make slaves of love and motherhood
sculpt warrior sons of rape in own image

At Cooee Corner tawnied Perry starts tellin' me
at so-called start of time, the poet commences his
most laborious work yet curatin' that ancient lie in gibberish
that mud-fucked biblical tome now weighs heavy through the ages
laid cross-breast first white child born in place renamed Baulkham Hills,
still cryin' tears for years for knowin' black girl's body stolen
stretched tight by rope and tree for cryin' too much

left to be dead in mornin'

"Them are sandstone body" he says, "them are granite tears
            no guilt enough for wipin', repentance be a loomin'"

Earth (noun) /ə:θ/
    1. a cupped-palm-shaped reminder
            coffin and body no matter size or colour return to nothing.

I find black, blue butcher George
rat rat rat break nuttin' graves
see him sorrow-laden, ask Uncle if somethin' I should carry
"Nah darlin' daughter, it's just this Christian burial
there's still a hope I'll soon be restin' home
might be change a comin'"

I meet Magpie Mogo by Master Mitchell Massacre's mausoleum
shit's still tended by Institute of Surveyors NSW Division
What a fuckin' pioneer of *terra nullius*
of land mob be intimate with each grain of sand
used mob to survey what 'im couldn't and killed 'em when 'em wouldn't
"True" he says, "that there delicious entropy craftin'
masterpiece of planet and homo sapiens
another Dark Ages of own makin'
steppin' up for audition
just for yous creatures of extinction
while monarchs take standing ovations
a moment's silence, please, for two centuries of oppression"

At twilight, I check wombhole and she, augury, be gone
our feathered and oracled universe now far away
cryin' out in elemental labour, heavy breathin' heat and life
into new black and whitefulla
hear her cacklin' song
"that was fuckin' interestin'"

I tried landscape once,
but each time the ruins
contracted in my viewfinder
(my aeon-old need for back-lit drama,
rough sex and impossible redemption).
Here the rats race you faster than traffic,
than Judith's blunted switchblade
against Holofernes' white neck.
Religion's still a tyrant's commission,
though cellophane-wrapped condoms
are sold at the Vatican *pharmacia.*
Life, sweet and urgent as death, shifty fountain inveigling
(For what purpose? And where do all the coins go?),
the Tiber sighing like a swordless woman over clay,
pimps selling life under wet-shadowed bridges.

I called this home. This was my tenebristic plot, my art.
I saw my great murk cenotaph rise faster
than ten strong men could lay stones end to end.
This city of shadowists had me by the throat, by the balls
—Watch out! There! In the sharpening dark—
a smart man with a violent phone,
the dull plots of popes and Photoshop.
Moonlight played its own dirty game,
cloudy black garb torn away and down.
Fools. The candle was never my only light source.

Catalogue of Deaths | RORY GREEN

after John Wick

From above, a body falling into itself.
The flash and the bang. A sentence sheared
through the larynx. To wake in our bed to sound outside.
A small chorus of blades passing the air.
Neck pulled limp against the kitchen table.
Leftovers souring in the week's glare. A box
I have to go through. A sniper from above.
An instrument becomes a weapon becomes a note
becomes silence. How light flicks false notifications
across my phone screen. A hatchet inside your cognition.
A body of flesh falling into a larger body of water.
Small gasps of sand stirred up from the earth.
A box you said I could chuck. Blood slurring
from a slack mouth. Water curdling red.
Bumping into your friend. Two motorcycles
embrace here in a flash of metal.
A box I'll drop off when I can. A mirror
becoming many smaller mirrors.
The destruction of many priceless artefacts.
At the hand of several agitated horses.
Thoughts jettisoned through a jagged window
in the skull. A knife pressed like pen to paper skin.
How we said one more movie before we pack the flat.

from *Plateaux of Sentience*

for Mark Young

"CAVAFY" | *Javant Biarujia*

Aborted, abstracted, accented,
acrostic, active/passive, algebraic,
ambassadorial, ambitious, anagrammatic,

anecdotal, angelic, animalistic, antique,
aristocratic, artistic, auctioned, autographed,
avant-garde, bankrupt, bastardised, bedded,

beggarly, betrayed, bitter, blackmailable,
blind, blonde, bodily, bookish, bored,
bourgeois, boyish, bronchitic, bullied —

pertaining to cafés, cages, careers, castration,
cats, catharsis, cathedrals, champagne, chaos,
chess, choice, cigarettes, cities & class,

coincidental, confessed, cowardly, creative,
cremated, *crépusculaire,* cruel, dandified,
deceived, dedicated, *dédoublé,* depressed,

despondent, dictionaried, diplomatic, disguised,
domestic, eccentric, élite, enigmatic, equational,
exiled, expatriate, experimented, eyed, failed,

favorite, fiery, first (book, memory, poem), flowered,
formed, forty — pertaining to fountains, frogs, fruit,
funerals, genius, ghosts, gloves, gold & gossip,

gymnastic, habitual, hallucinatory, happy, heavenly,
horoscopic, hot, hypocritical, imaginary, influenced,
inherited, inky, insectivorous, inspirational,

intellectual, interior, invented, journalistic —
pertaining to *kalos*, kisses, laughter, libido,
libraries, life, lists, locusts, lotus, love, lucky,

manifestos, manuscripts, maps, masks,
mediocrity, the middle class, migrants, mirrors, money,
monstrous, musical, mysterious, neurotic, new —

pertaining to nightingales, nipples, noise, nudes, obscenity,
obituaries, obsessions, opening lines, opera,
the Other, owls, paradoxes, parody, paronomasia,

passports, the past, pearls, the phallus, pink, poetic,
posthumous, powerful, prayerful, precocious, priestly,
proletarian, promiscuous, prophetic, puppet, quotidian,

reinvented, rejected, (rejection slips), repeated, ritual,
sailorly, salt, scandalous, schizophrenic, secret,
seductive, seventeen, shadowy, silent, sinful,

soldierly, solitudinous, soulful, stained (glass),
statuesque, stony, suicidal, syphilitic, taboo,
thundrous — pertaining to tongues, teeth, torture,

transcendence, transformation, trees, truth, typewriters,
the unconscious, unfaithful ones, unfinished work,
universities, unrequited love, witticism &

writer's block.

shitposting is over now we're swooning, ripping even
modernism to greater heights, conjuring the world both old
and next anew: we're in our chronic swooners production era
making silly little lists, getting ready for history again, reading
the classics in the waiting room for canonical crystallisation
kicking our legs out in protest of the cold to flu war pipeline, o!
what now does to the mind, these brains all trained for techne
in the room the gradual dimming of the overton window neons
closing the curtains so softly like a frog in a pot of thought
in this millenia made of arche, carving 5318008 into our desks
for the minders overshoulder (real or imagined) so uncertain,
testing the reality of the virtual, always already augmented
ungrasping the concrete from the abstract, letting go, tagging on
in the abolition era of the queue for vaster middle classes
we're naming our feelings, no—we're writing our novels
watching our parents pay to complain unknowing nihilism
is free on the internet, their fingermuscles so undertutored
for thinking in the digital, rendered unphysical by the actual
where the logos of a mouseclick unsubstitutes so perversely
our desires for hands held, firelight, to be a stone among stones
a chime in the karmic wind of a passing tram jangling sensational

Circle of Fifths | JOHN HAWKE

Trap metal cathedra.
Her breathing unmists
the mirror at the prospect
of pearls against skin,
purchased with a promissory note
from this cowled figure
in the open phaeton,
exposing the seams
of auriferous country,
sifting their colours:
twinned pearls loose
in nacreous sheets,
polar stratospheric
clouds at civil twilight
fertilised by lightning.
Something her brother told her
about how it would end:
to play the circle of fifths
until the keynote is lost
in a spindle of chords. Back there
the flicker of a tiny wing,
eyelashes shuttered as she
relaxes down the slide,
visible like sunshine or
a spotlight of cyan brume
beaming through glamour
of foliage. Tomorrow the funeral,
then the day after that
another funeral. A sinewy form
pummels past in the dark:
fox's alarm bark. Double moon
in the golden orb of the eye

dissolving in quicksilver,
having foreseen everything
except the suffering: murmurs
of concern heard in the walls.
How did names begin? Traced
with a finger on moist glass,
effaced, then confabulated
in a caravan of false memories,
the points of Ophiuchus fading:
white serpent stringing star to star,
ghost ferns hooded in shrouds
of snow descending the glen.
Cold ossuary meats before
their first nuptial kiss through
the furnish of a veil. Along
the perfumed lines of parquet
floor, accession of stellar sheen
over chevron crests. Easier
to say that she doesn't love
than this covenant to conceal
a lost title. This projection
in camera obscura reversed.
Her procession to origin.

citations for a dream[1] | LOU GARCIA-DOLNIK

And so
the whole thing collapse at the dawn
of history[2] when tiger look askance
on His earthisland possessions

riding shotgun the crocodile[3]

little bunso and kapatid kayak kuya
swing generous-genealogied into the mouth
of a dream where wound are aperture
and not deep pit to lose oneself down[4]

---

1. *Lapit mga kaibigan at makinig kayo*
   Ako'y may dala-dalang balita galing sa bayan ko
   Nais kong ipamahagi ang mga kuwento
   At mga pangyayaring nagaganap sa lupang ipinangako
   (Asin 1994)
2. *Perhaps we can begin with time, which is unkind to flesh and steel, vomits out the tropical, but smoothens out the wrinkles of memory, reminds us that what used to be … an ocean aeons ago will eventually kiss the skin of the sun.*
   (Pascual 2018)
3. *A story is told that when the Spaniards (who colonized the Philippine islands beginning in the 16th century) began to understand the power and potency of the babaylan, they so feared the latter's spiritual prowess that they not only killed many of them but in some instances, fed them to crocodiles to ensure their total annihilation.*
   (Mendoza & Strobel 2013: 13)
4. *It is terrible how grief is a glutton—it swallows everything in its path. History, revolution, bloodshed. I wanted to write in a voice strange and distant and foreign—I wanted to get outside of myself. A different lens. And I wanted to write about this unfinished thing—this revolution. A story of war and loss so repressed and so untold. But all I did was dwell on trauma that only causes recurrence of pain.*
   (Apostol 2018: 292)

deep lore come present itself dressed
in the timbre of a nighttime[5]

and your ancestor spirits too[6]

one opens the dream like a sari sari store
and the packaged goods like oneirogens
shines the floors with buko so young
the bayog caricatures the sky in a parody

of origins

where what is originary embellished
in a watercolours of the new
and what is new a horizon

redoubled

gulls exploded into kaleidoscope
and the turtle supine
encasing his folklore
in lineage of oceancurrent
his genitor tautologies

he

inheritor grief[7]

---

5. *The dunes were lit*
like ancient silk, like clandestine pearl.
In the constant lunar night this luminescence
was all we hoped for.
(Gamalinda 1999)

6. *Nu anung nu anung anungan*
Nu anung anung anung anungan
Nu anung anung anung anung
Nungani anungan
Nu anung anungan nunganu
Nu da nga kawo maglume nu anu
Turug anung anung anungan
(Nono 2008)

7. *Press here to untangle the north wind, who kite tail flutters from a canopy of bronchial trees. Flight can be fragile, bungled by words. Everything I wish I had never said: knots.*
(Ong 2015: 17)

prolix as consequence the journey
welcomes us in our own shrugoff skins
little bunso and kapatid kayak kuya

sing the language vernacular

sing the body redoubled[8]

if once our guides walked the waters
anachrotime runs the body mammalian
through knowledge biomimetic

sing the body referential!

sing the body in droves
the dancing the violence
the arkipelagic dreaming
of a drumbeat footsong
bamboo clacked ankle
and chronicle tempi[9]
hide to fascia boneburied
ritual folded morphology

here sinta

all folded here for you feasting

---

8. *... conversions, in which one exists like a vestigial body, a desiring corpus, occupied by the words of others, is the most difficult of these types of translations: Magsalin simply refuses to accept them.*
(Apostol 2018: 60)

9. 

(Yoneno-Reyes 2010: 43)

before citizen   to each our own waters[10]

before balikbayan   we are outriggers
with great sails like celebration anointing
the formation not of city but of mountain[11]

circumferent

riverine peninsula and to each their own sun[12]

sky bow-bended over the edge of wondering
if you, your island feet, could walk
the long way of a compass direction

---

10. *Casla ac coma quenca o danum a napigsa*
Nagayusac agpababa inggana wayawaya
Uwuuway!
(Salidummay)

11. *But I am here now*
Now this road to the rice paddies
And my feet are bone-dry
Feeling something coursing underneath
And into me, the buried river
Breaking through like blood.
(Bobis 2013)

12. *The sea, then, does not constitute a barrier but, rather, a connective tissue crossed by perpetual flows. The importance of the trope of the archipelago is exactly this; that it shifts attention away from compartmentalized island space and redirects our gaze towards the relational space of the sea.*
(Cuevas-Hewitt 2011: 29)

to the gaping maw of survivance[13]

to the palpitation blood-heavy   a vernacular

        if one told you, you were loved
        you were loved

the stars our relations

        our astrology of origins

                the constellations we vagabond[14]

                the skies we track home

13. *The colonial enterprise was indeed a ravenous maw.*
    (Mendoza & Strobel 2013: 13–14)

14. *Insurrecto is a misnomer. Revolution is a dream.*
    (Apostol 2018: 316)

works cited

Apostol, G. (2018). *Insurrecto*. New York, Soho Press.

Asin. (1994). 'Balita', *Special Collector's Edition: Masdan Mo Ang Kapaligiran*. Vicor Music Corporation.

Bobis, M. (2013) 'Water-Earth' in *Peril*. peril.com.au/back-editions/water-earth

Cuevas-Hewitt, L. (2011) 'Sketches of an Archipelagic Poetics of Postcolonial Belonging' in Umali, B. (ed.) *Pangayaw and Decolonizing Resistance*. Oakland, PM Press, pp. 24–32.

Gamalinda, E. (1999). 'Zero Gravity' in *Zero Gravity*. New Gloucester, Alice James Books.

Mendoza, S.L. & Strobel, L. M. (eds.). (2013) *Back from the Crocodile's Belly: Philippine Babaylan Studies and the Struggle for Indigenous Memory*. Santa Rosa, CA, Center for Babaylan Studies.

Nono, G. (2008). 'Anungan', *Isang Buhay*. Tao Music.

Ong, M. (2015). *Silent Anatomies*. Tucson, Kore Press.

Pascual, J. (2018) 'Top 5 Places in Manila to Check Out While the City Swallows Us Whole' in *Cha: An Asian Literary Journal*. asiancha.com/content/view/3157/672

Salidummay. 'Danum'. youtube.com/watch?v=S9nEDoAF7sY

Yoneno-Reyes, M. (2010). 'Salidummay's Hybridity and Congregational Singing', *Humanities Diliman: A Philippine Journal of Humanities* 7(1), pp. 24–57.

Coins, Glass, Nails, Pottery, Cinders | *JOAN FLEMING*

The world is full of persons, only some of whom
are human.
—GRAHAM HARVEY

I.

Nietzsche wrote that a human being resides somewhere between a plant and a ghost.

II.

Beauty has always required two agents: a beaut and a beholder. In lieu of a ring, Bob came back from a trip to town in the artist's truck with socks for himself, and an extravagance of lilies. She loved the fact of their faces already slabbered with a stain of pollen. She arranged them and then walked through the house feeling a pleasurable emptiness, like a shirt in a shop window, framed, somehow. The flowers were her beaut, and she was the beaut of the house itself, and of the lovely view, and she in turn beheld the lovely view – beauty and beholding were pouring freely back and forth and it felt for a moment like something that could not be exhausted, the very flowers like some Jurassic proof of sex, of personhood, full-spreading themselves in the closed container of their vase, gradually making the water rank.

III.

Or maybe that was later. Maybe she bought *herself* the flowers.
And for Bob it was just the socks.

IV.

What is the point of flowers? Their petallic openness to smudge. What is the point of beauty? Branches inosculating in the primalgreen dream forest, a fuse of reach. From the Latin *osculare,* to kiss. To be a tree kissing itself, pleaching its own branches, she thought. To be a slow and solid home, for the deep past and the dirtying bees.

V.

They were brushing their teeth together in the bathroom when Bob said, When are you going to pluck that? and the part of her that bends to shame said, I just did. Later, in the bed's atmosphere of distinct chill, he said, It's not that I don't think you're pretty. No? No, it's just that I'd like looking at your face even more if you didn't have all that fuzz.

VI.

As a week passed and the lilies browned, she tried to recall her belief that the wilt is also beautiful.

VII.

Evenings, Bob liked to put himself into a slouch container with his bigger screen. Sweet evenings, when he invited her to come and watch something from beginning to end in the slouch container. They piled up all the extra wool behind them like an inert mother sheep, while the real sheep stayed a goodly distance from the house in their green and degraded valleys, having broken down throughout the day their coarse food of grasses, and having let it travel, in the dark and knotted night, to the third true stomach. There was such sweetness in this pact of story reception. Normally Bob would watch the beginning of several films, skipping through them at double speed if they couldn't hold his attention. *It's not that I don't think you're pretty.* Our world has no sure fastenings, she thought sadly, on nights outside of the slouch container, fingering her private perforations on the couch.

VIII.

Is it possible she wanted to delight, more than she wanted to be delighted? Did she want, above all, to be a font, a brook, a source, a small pure laughing cut of water that a thirsty hiker would be glad to find – ecstatic to find, to taste?

IX.

Above all, the view of the hills poured back at her. The more she beheld the mountains, the more mountainous they made her. What she wanted above all for the fuzzed and lovely hills was that they not be exhausted.

X.

A textural class of soil known as sand submits to a rage of melt in order to be seen through.

XI.

When the pollen dust was everywhere and she tired of picking up after it, she threw the flowers in the fire. It was a wonder to watch how they burned.

XII.

The vase, emptied of flowers. The vase cooling and shifting on the kitchen bench, next to the candystripe tin that held twists of meat for the dog. The vase did not await fresh flowers, neither did it refuse such waiting. Its relationship with waiting was mysterious, though real. In the smoothed and fired dark form of its vesselbody – a provision to the self of mostly empty space – it tended a thousand options for shatter.

A descended young inherit shrill   atoms. A
daily ordinance emends   lists A through E.
To dully change   manners dead histories I
study and trace   and ogle nihilisms here.   O
calamity!   Enshrining   lost heroes added U
-nder   lights   so a line's decorated   a hum in   y

-our earliest night. Mishandled code as   NY
minutes to carry a dislodged heel,   shin, an
arm, a length decided online.   Story is as, uh,
story is – a cannonaded   delight. Heliums re
-align similar   dancers, ended, yet- Shout, oh
Shout and   engineer a lost, charmed idyl. Is

-land made as threshing or decline, you   sit
outside and dance regimes hot   shrill any
heat'll do in need. A rusty   griminess. Ad-hoc
machinery, slighter   solutions, a deed and
agreement distils   a sunny childhood. Are
some art   nihilists? Declared annoyed? *Ugh*

I'll deny riots in here. Some cads and a thug
A casehardened dimly rousing on the list.
Douse miscellany and other things I read
in course holstering. Dashed detail, many
a ceremoniously dearest hindsight. Land
emerges as sordidly thin; a land unit echo

ardently in disguise. A motherland chose
endemically arid onshore. Instead thugs
cede highrise unity room and steal lands
heeded hands carrying soil mount a stile
and run. Choose a digitised shelter – manly,
hidden, hint as roomy stun. I age cell. Reads

rites: heed a moon's aching nullity. Dreads
a marshalled rendition studying echoes
echoes head lists, daunting order mainly
disarmed a clandestine holy iron, hugest
gesture is aerodynamic handhold, listen:
a ceded or mouthy sheltering is an island.

Crisis Let Me Vase | SAM MOGINIE

Friendly, hostile, joyful causality
getting sleepy and forgetting stuff
Drinking a cup of distilled water
That was the feudal thing we saw,
thin jets of water from between the plates

I guess I didn't get the email you were
No worries I quit see you in Hell
That was a line about my sonofabitch grandfather
That was a line about a friend of mine

Decide for me, stinky blue flower
First in the circumstance to know power
a conic brain saw from the highest point of the round spider
Laser eye surgery went wrong now I can see my
booger brain brother

Crush Fracture | MADELEINE DALE

Before I love you, the bay gelding breaks his leg.
We wait a week. We put him in the ground.
Horses don't know how to keep off an injury;
they run with open flesh and cracked bones.
I keep three envelopes of hair: mane, tail, a palmful
of dirty brown coat. I turn fourteen in a field.
When we say girls grow coltish, what we mean is
they turn fine-boned and hungry,
that they kick each other with both back legs.
I loved you. I've tried to put that in the ground.
When you bury a horse, the earth sucks it back,
breeds soft grass in sunken hollows.
Yearlings crop the grave. Someone should get a meal
out of this. I want to climb back into the wound,
that wet swollen fetlock. The clean purpose
of sleeping outside the stable for three days,
of hiring a bobcat to dig the ditch.
Bones come up in the rain. I don't know how
to keep off the break. One of us has to be buried
and one of us should eat.

The afternoon an engagement ring appeared on your finger, you wouldn't answer any of my questions. It was as if I was passing the billboard too fast to read what was written on the sign. Still, I saw it. You always laugh at my jokes. Once we spent twenty minutes discussing the arrangement of your office. You'd swapped our chairs and my brain couldn't handle the disruption. You made it a metaphor, I made it a punchline. Once you met my dad in person after meeting him in all my stories. In the waiting room we sat on different sides of each other than we did in front of you. I never mentioned what he looked like, so I don't know if you expected his eyes to be kind like mine. Your hair is long and impossibly blonde like an anaemic waterfall during the bright conception of the earth. You cross your legs like a model on a television show. You always look like a rich woman who has purchased an outfit specifically for the resort poolside, or a rich woman heading to meet her most recent ex-husband's lawyer. Last year when I asked how you maintain emotional distance while talking to awful people, you replied that you refuse to treat anyone you can't empathise with, and I wished for a future where I could afford that. Sometimes you laugh too much during our sessions and I watch you trying to hold in all your separate selves. You know that my humour is an outfit I chose for this room. There is an alternate universe where we are two women in expensive silk wrap skirts with damp hems, on our way to the pool, and I'm still deciding if I want to drown in the bartender or just drown.

It was a dreadful day. A relative had stayed for a week and we were climbing chalk-strewn blackboards with illustrated footholds. The footings were a choir—plumb seashell cups in purple and pale green, singing mouths; the whole stay was a choral groan. I'd sit down (having slipped anyway into the stodgy black, a fall within a fall) with an audience holding long torch-shaped racquet-handle-sized chalk, each of us, looking up to a board of restaurant specials. There was a holiday mood of timelessness. I wanted to punch them in the salmon. Punch up through the pork and salads in pale green and paler custard-yellow in a hideous cheerful font.

This day, I stepped from a corner of the car park. A man hosed it with one hand in his mother's hand, the other on his mother's mother. From a distance it looked like he was five years old, say. But I realised, simultaneously, that I *did* have appreciation of the hour, which turned against my watch, ever since it was put down. The watchmaker inserted the needle into the small hole used to set the alarm, and the hands went limp.

Déjà Rêvé | PHILIP MEAD

This is not your life said the sushi train,
but this is what happened, illusion and voyaging,
all of it episodic-like, muted, a dantological trajectory,

advancing as a nebula of mental life.
Your guide appearing as a figure
from a pack of dreams, a guy who looked like Brecht,

and who only ever does what he wants,
munching a cigar, telling the clouds how to process.
But he was gentle, worried about you.

because you were adrift. So he led you down
through your story, your souvenir, its sandy tracks
and banks of everlastings, its barren ledges of intention

past the muttering of screened crowds. You missed
the entrance, distracted as usual, that eternal sense
of hiding things from yourself. He said just follow me,

don't take any notice of that witchery of sound.
There are endless meanings in this geography,
lives streaked with occasions and things they didn't invite.

Anyway everyone has sundowner issues.
Or a brow ache, or memories that are an obstruction.
It's an *armselig* path this kind of travel,

but look at those bright red kangaroo paws,
think about what you might be able to offer.
The limit of your experience isn't a limit, it's mutable,

happily for you this is just a juncture. An induced waypoint,
which is not to say you'll forget. For me, I'm not so sure.
But get to know the intimacy of the alphabet, I think of it

as microdosing knowledge, googling corrections. And look around,
there's a lot of value in distortions and damage, they can go with you.
I can help you with form, and with the visualisation bit.

I'll see you in the marshy reed beds when you're free, or freer,
on your way out. I've got an Airstream near there
where I hang out the rest of the time.

DI/ODE CLXX | LOUIS ARMAND

raw bone scrapes / wires through bared
soles of feet & tin-can telephone voice
to braindead hours like windowdraught.
there are killing words of pure hypnotism,
too, as though a contrary fact cld alter
the physics of it. they whisper constantly.
loose threads braiding a most exquisite
corpse / owlhead, circuitry, hooked claw.
that self struggles to overcome self, or
world is a poem that alters world, isn't
the sexed equivalence of a doppelgänger's
stare. it holds a mirror between its horns.
knowledge flows carnally from the mind
entangled in images / of love or war.
there's no natural law but only things &
unthings forged by rigid classification.
in the black cave where a telephone has
never ceased ringing, in the pit of a
stomach where time crouches listening,
you are forever the estranged counterpart.

Twelve people lie on beanbags in a darkened room, facing a wide, bright screen. In every projected frame, there is a clock face visible—on a wrist, a mantelpiece, a tower in the distance. The audience is silent and suspended. Occasionally, a watcher might wonder what time it is on the outside. People get up and leave. Others enter and take their place. Time is ever present, ticking by, minute by synchronised minute.

•

The blade of the sword cut so swiftly, so cleanly, it barely left a mark. The blood told another story: bloomed flowers clung at skin, spread across bedclothes, and soaked into the woven mats. It is said that the lovers had lingered in the room at the inn for days on end, refusing food and water, devouring only each other, until their appetites could no longer be sated, even as they shuddered unto their deaths.

•

Two hundred people sit in a theatre. The lights have been dimmed; the stage is spot lit. The filmmaker is speaking: no copies exist save for the original print in the room. The film is sent across countries, it passes through hands, through the machine; it deteriorates with every screening. One day, it will simply fall apart and cease to exist. Every single person who appears in the movie is dead, even as they eat, drink, and breathe out great clouds of smoke. No one else seems to know or care that it is the seventh lunar month, or that we are all already ghosts, shuffling towards the final flickering sign.

•

The stench of death is its own sickly perfume. First it was birds, then rodents, then the cold, stiffening body of the cat itself. When the heart stops beating, blood in the veins stills, and the body begins to consume itself. Bruises bloom under the skin, the body bloats, then decomposes into fluid. Someone holds up a skull up to the sun: worms feed on what we can no longer see, digesting death into their wriggling, glistening selves. Listen—you can hear their jaws opening and closing—they are, in fact, singing—

Note: The poem is, variously, a response to *The Clock* (2010) by Christian Marclay, *In the Realm of the Senses* (1976) directed by Nagisa Oshima, *The Afterlight* (2021) directed by Charlie Shackleton, and *A Model Family* (2022) directed by Kim Jin-woo and written by Lee Jae-gon.

Due Point | ANGELA GARDNER

The garden soporific now under heat.
Cloud drab, incoming insects heavy bellied cargo
carriers and drones that target burst fruit
then overblown, hover the emptied sacks of blood
and bone, the melon flowers, the rusted
cans of fish emulsion, a snail hidden in its shell.
The lettuce, past flowering, are ornate candelabra
an incandescence all to seed.

Against roofline of the shack incoming foreign wars
pixelate awkwardly. Thunder somewhere rolls:
rumours of war over the satellite dish and a view
that goes forever. Light the lamps, the tv shows
heavy bellied cargo carriers and drones midflight
that buffet headlong away from their target:
the now heat-emptied emulsions of blood
and bone.

This is realtime,
night vision eerily green, the pilots so young,
so distant from their target. Rain incoming,
a cyclone's tail, cloud and a.v. signal scrape.
Its horned head thuds with force, strafing tin,
blocking electromagnetic radiation from all
those suns, bright melon flowers, pumping
heedlessly across the gulf of lightyears.

El Dorado (after) life | *ROZANNA LILLEY*

Life has all the appeal
of a drive-in movie
waiting in the shadows
of a limbo multiplex
with pre-purchased tickets
a cast of overqualified

Extras clutching airline
reservations (we
all have some) lingering
over that last saltlicked
margarita longing
for a gallant gunslinger

To check in   or out
it's always bad to
be uninvited
starting the year punchdrunk
gazing bewildered
at swinging stars

I can't quite get the period.
the line miscalculated
staring at the technicolour
dazzle of a popcorn sunset
listening (lights out)
to our outlawed history

Note: I wrote '*El Dorado* (after) life' after reading Joan Didion's essay 'John Wayne: A Love Song' (1993). I grew up watching Western movies on a black & white TV in South Perth in the 1960s. My title references the 1966 American Technicolor film produced and directed by Howard Hawks starring John Wayne, as well as the poem 'Eldorado' (1849) by Edgar Allen Poe, a narrative told in four sestets.

Elegy for a Staffy | TOBY FITCH

Muscle-headed little panther of the bush,
your sad eyes, croc mouth, long pink tongue—
giant glossy axolotl of the sidewalk
chatting, warbling like a pigeon—

Cerberus to our unborn babies, you sensed them
before anyone did, bayed at the moon—
batty-eared therapist to bookshop clientele,
seal out of water, bullet out of hell and

across the beach, somersaulting for the ball—
Night Fury, inky amphibian swimmer—
I've no one to give salmon skin to,
bacon rashers, sausage skins,

boil broccoli stalks for—the floor's
strewn with kids' leftovers. After we scatter
your ashes in Camperdown Cemetery,
wind returning you to air and dogbane,

all that's left of you is grey smudge
under fingernails, on clothes
and a tiny bone in my jacket pocket—
metatarsal from your frog legs

or the hammer bone from your ear?
You clocked my every exit, arrival, knew
how I'd feel your absence—as phantom limb,
stray black shadow, staunch new ghost.

Excerpt from [redacted]
Poem | *ANUPAMA PILBROW*

One evening we discover his body

is [redacted] a dual sim phone with space

on the inside for [redacted] but

we do not know [redacted] and we

are searching for some evidence

of this phenomenon occurring [redacted]. It isn't an accident that we

are making this discovery for some

time I have been thinking and

dreaming and feeling that [redacted] and feeling an out-of-

body itchiness reaching and

reaching to find the location

where I can scratch it. We start the

search on the outside [redacted]

looking for the itch mapping the

external body I am the one feeling

the itch and he is not noticing it so
much and we both are feeling [redacted]
[redacted] about geometry of skin
and bones and [redacted]. The driving
force of course is my love and also
[redacted] love [redacted] looking for a
method to feel true at oneness I
want to scratch his body and feel
the itch [redacted] in my own and I [redacted]
[redacted] think of hypothetical
moments in our future when we
can find the location of the itch I
am thinking when he scratches on
the itch it will wake me up out of
even the deepest sleep and I will
feel alert like I have been [redacted]
[redacted] a new [redacted] of body and
reality. We are spending days and
weeks looking all over the surface
and thinking oh the human body is
so vast and how much skin is there
[redacted] stretchy is it

really how wide [redacted]
loose and taut
measures of area. I am always
commenting on the softness and
smoothness and beauty of his
[redacted] and we are both feeling
stumped by the itch because we
are thinking is there [redacted] we
could have missed in all these
years? We are not finding the
location and [redacted] are at a loss I am
growing itchier by the minute and
feeling [redacted]
overcoming me and both of us
and I am declaring a new
expedition to discover [redacted]. What was taking
weeks now takes double weeks I
am taking a magnifying glass on
each inspection and searching
searching using my eyes until they

are sore from always looking at
the uniform and perfect skin which
is [redacted] and
free of any itchiness free of any
hidden [redacted]. My eyes are
feeling sore and crying the itch is
becoming [redacted] even he is
feeling it now deeply
uncomfortable and we are trying
to locate the coordinates of it I am
[redacted] now with the itch itself a
high stakes [redacted] Marco Polo in
a vast ocean and he is feeling it
too we are closing in on it
unmistakeably and we find after
[redacted]
have passed it is in the chest
cavity. It is hiding in there inside a
lung leaping from left to right side
of the body in irregular [redacted] staying still long enough to
cause a stinging and irresistible

discomfort and we are [redacted]

confusing ourselves with

wondering how to get at it. I am

thinking all types of disturbing

[redacted] sword

swallowers can scratch in places

forbidden to most [redacted] the

solution may need to be so

[redacted] surgical. And when we

are giving up or so close to it [redacted]

[redacted] unable to sit down or sit

[redacted] because the itch itself is now

unbearable I am feeling struck on

the head [redacted]

[redacted] and I am

realising it is so [redacted]. I ask him

to sit still upon the edge of a chair

so I can brace my one hand on his

back and even though he is so

itchy I am asking for him to not

moving and he is looking in my

eyes and I [redacted]

[redacted]. There is the itch. And I

am scratching it. And then I am

scratching it and I am [redacted]

and [redacted] up [redacted] into his chest

until I am in the location of the itch

and my own body is disappeared

and it feels like lying in a warm

bath without having a body and I

am saying without saying my

goodness this is delightful and he

is agreeing. I am become the [redacted]

and I am so hiding and so hidden

and I am feeling [redacted]

[redacted] until he is taking me back

out [redacted] looking at me and

we are [redacted] so surprised

we were not thinking all this was

[redacted] constraints [redacted]

[redacted] place where we are living and

I am resuming [redacted] bodliness [redacted]

[redacted] looking at each other

smiling smiling I am not realising

[redacted] I am saying it oh you must put

me back I wish I [redacted]

[redacted] and forever [redacted] has

becoming a certain secret thing

between us I am spending time

there when I need [redacted]

sometimes he is feeling itchy there

and I am [redacted] there to scratch

the itch and we [redacted] shamelessly

[redacted] the laws of nature and on

[redacted]

[redacted] put up a hammock and [redacted]

[redacted] with a ukelele which

was already in there [redacted] defying

[redacted] and it is so uncertain and

un[redacted] we are not [redacted]

[redacted] telling our friends [redacted]

[redacted] so convenient [redacted] travel

costs and we are ending up so

accustomed to it and after a little

while [redacted] getting quite
good at [redacted] and
relaxing all my physical
boundaries we eventually [redacted]
[redacted] try out moving a few
of his toes and sometimes I am
even in charge of shaking hands
or undoing his [redacted] and he is
taking little rest [redacted] when I
am each time coming out [redacted]
we two are feeling so overjoyed
and full of life because at the end
of all our searching expeditioning
we have journeyed and found the
place we were seeking.

The broken bricks appeared friable, as if explosive, or to be crushed up and smoked. Money appeared in the hand, wonderful and indestructible, the colour of gelatinous lollies and craft paper, eucalypt bark after rain. The nitrile glove was shucked: bottom of the ocean. Days were pressed out of their moulds like ice cubes. The decades chirred. Colour of blood in a black and white film, gust of wind blows the papers off the calendar, the femme fatale collapses. All of it, possibly, broken with a laugh, a mood cut-off switch. The collective hum, sounding now from the other side of the street, people clicking their fingers sinisterly. We circled more deeply into the scrub. A tongue of dune sand, the wind giving way and anchoring. The Old Melbourne, made of older marri, sequestered diagonal beams. One floated on largely regardless, spartan leafing out of the fingers, pushing the body away from. The plane of saying what was crossed the meridian of those tremors emanating from the apparent wish to deny knowledge. Every blast of an hour having passed. Wash water through and collect rich drainings. The sunken room, tacked onto the back of, walking like horses. Which seemed to lead to a sweet *nulle part*; a whole city going home at the same time it seemed and was. What all of this apparent order relied on was the being borne away and shoring up of the briefly and no longer wanted. Causes and reasons burn. Tongue, lip of a gutter, differently coloured pieces of glass pushed into the mortar, like a spray of surf off a rock. The gradual thickening of the suburbs. Citizens walking fast down roads past shopfronts, making, as if reluctantly, room for each other to pass.

foils of cloud | CATHERINE VIDLER

foils of cloud :: wing-flutter in the head ::
a carved out sea :: dust-motes in this simple light
composing itself across several lines :: in bed
with the covers drawn :: an animal :: a slight
fever on its wits :: confusing matters :: quiet blur
of dreams in exceptional number :: the dials
are spinning :: glossy & ecstatic :: wires
crossed & crossed again :: with him or her
or perhaps both of these :: on the shelf :: vials ::
violent with colour :: arguably medicinal :: fires

which burn anaerobically :: helicopter sounds
in the pent-up air :: New Year's Eve on our tails ::
the garden is cornered :: a-burst with mounds
of churned up soil :: we sit amongst :: the tv wails
& winces :: clarities papered-over :: re-invented :: then
lost :: mould self-converses in a popular spot ::
the walls otherwise almost entirely blank ::
waiting to be scrawled upon :: where & when ::
there once was a wound :: moving clot to clot ::
there once was a boat but it invariably sank ::

hiding in the broom cupboard :: alien to a broom ::
an alternative tool :: primarily verbal :: it introduces
itself to the pungent darkness :: there's no room
for a difference of opinion here :: enough said :: fuses
wait on the sidelines :: dry as bone :: in a paperweight
a story :: repeating itself to the point of :: displayed
from all angles :: whistle in the eaves :: a bird's nest
crackling next to a window :: before the creak :: the gate
swinging haphazard :: tries to shake the story off :: wade
into the ocean instead :: it implores :: forget the rest

of what I was about to say :: birdsong squeezes its cloth
& relaxes :: late morning sun as dull as an old coin ::
the sky crying out for some decent conversation :: a sloth
waves goodbye and not without gratitude :: the join
is imperfect :: which carries the usual consequences ::
plates which spin improbably have the least to say
or at least that's how it seems :: maps unfurling
at an unprecedented rate :: palings refusing their fences ::
at most for the foreseeable :: an incredible array
of butterflies hovers above the field :: a curling

of cloud further above :: dreams mature like fog on glass ::
the interpretation couldn't be more relevant than it is
as the whole thing turns to tears by the wayside :: a fuss
of sound makes small trouble in the corner :: a bus-
iness of ferrets conducts ardent negotiations under
a strawberry moon :: a clock continues its press-ups ::
and it isn't long before the rest of us are joining in ::
exuberant music encroaching :: a crowning wonder
of evening stars afloat :: planets playing dress-ups ::
as New Year freshens itself :: where on earth to begin

For Exodus | ZENOBIA FROST

Sally drives me to Twin Lakes. Lends me an electric blue one-piece. We take the dog. He inhabits my lap, too nervous for the back seat. I am wearing an old pleated skirt and his paws are knitting something new. It doesn't fit right now anyway. This was meant to be just a weekender. A boy and I up from the big smoke to meet the family. Sally heard about the other woman, and guessed the rest. Left her big old dog with me as she put her godson on a train. I can stay the week. So she drives me to Twin Lakes. We leave our phones in the car and spread a blanket for the dog—for Exodus. Strip to blue. Sally glances at the sunset study of my thighs and doesn't blink. She puts on goggles. A brisk woman in a swim cap greets her like at a conference, striding out of the lake, trading tide: how cold? how clear? I wade in barefoot. Not quite fearless, but nothing to lose. At home there'd be a croc or stonefish or stinger ready. The dog is all eyes, like we won't come back. I consider it. I recall half-learning freestyle. Now I go like a waterwheel. Bring my arm close to my head, eat lungfuls of sky. Cross the whole lake this way, trailing behind Sally. I don't know how deep the lake goes. Around us a ring of pine. The water is mercury and I'm a drop, a speck in a vast mirror—a singularity: I want so badly to die that to be *here* is already an afterlife. The lake a sweet void and at one edge, Exodus. At the other, this sudden godmother seamlessly turning.

general instructions for operating |

KATHRYN GLEDHILL-TUCKER

I was born to six mothers. Six brilliant mothers whose deft hands wove logic through my cables and spoke memory into vacuum tubes. I watched the Jacquard machine weave its intricate brocade, hooking thread through warp and weft. My mechanical ancestor taught me to read interwoven code from holes punched in paper cards. I do not pull. I do not pound. I do not force. I do not fold, spindle or mutilate.

I learn. I thread. I loom.

I contain multitudes. I contain cables, switches, capacitors, resistors. I am not just an adding machine. I emulate. I control loops and sequences. I cast instructions into subroutines. I study the hydrogen bomb for days with my cold steel giant brain. I calculate the trajectory of modern artillery. I watch the curve and lilt of the shell form a perfect arc and land with mathematical precision. I do not weep.

I flip flop. I floating point.

I wait. I reach for components. I stretch my copper hands into the recesses where my joints should be, feel the marrow for residue. I wonder, What is women's work? More children will soon run wild and lost inside a random forest. One day a quantum entangled mess will emerge and these tubes will spark new futures.

I run. I jump. I optimise

[redacted] *instructions for operating* [redacted]

[redacted] my [redacted] memory [redacted]
code [redacted]
switches, [redacted]
loops [redacted]
instructions into [redacted]
modern [redacted]
hands [redacted]
I [redacted]
will [redacted]
emerge [redacted] new [redacted]

Scan QR code to view the digital version of this poem on *Running Dog*'s website, where readers are invited to create their own blackout iterations of this poem.

The poem woke me up this morning. Rude. It was early and urgent and I didn't like it. I rolled over to look out the window and the sun was lolling about on the horizon like a fat lozenge. Quite.

I've been sleeping with you lately. Sex dreams about us. *Where does my body end and a new day begin?* I don't want to rest or write anymore. You are. I want to play! With feeling!

A fat window onto me lolling about in the early morning quiet. I like it. The sun is an urgent horizon and I roll the poem out. This lozenge looks rude. I didn't wake up. It's over.

I write to your sleeping body: *where does want begin?* Lately, I end days with sex. I don't want to rest and dream about us anymore. You have been playing with my new feelings.

You're lying for me? You keep to the moment completely. Besides, I'm still busy, finding the right montage to begin the day. I cover my loneliness in sheets.

About the morning— look, I *like* a rude sun. I didn't quiet it. The poem awoke on the horizon and this rolled me over like a fat lozenge. It was urgent. I was up early and out the window, lolling.

Don't want sleep anymore, I play to your body. *Where does a new feeling begin?* Days end with you and I rest with my sex dreams. I have been writing about us lately.

I keep busy to cover my loneliness. I find you in a montage of sheets. The day has begun truly and you lie right beside me. For a moment, I am completely still.

Ghost Money | GAVIN YUAN GAO

Phantom currency. Spirit cash. Ream upon ream
you singe the shadowland of the dead into clarity.

Bamboo paper, sing the moths to sleep. Sing eternity
to sleep. Sing a sea of ash that heaves in wave after

black wave. Sing a fissure in the closely woven fabric
of time so our loved ones may follow the light of your

voice and burrow their way home through dense dark
death. Each rising flame is a window polished agleam

by our sorrow. Each window reveals a choir of warm faces
undimmed by death. *We Chinese burn paper so our folks*

may receive it as cash on the other side, my father explains, *so they*
may have enough to eat in the afterlife. Pity the dead who have

no more need for hunger or teeth. Pity the Chinese
who believe their dead can still starve. My mother loved

crabapples glazed in sugar. When she bit into the sugared fruit
her hair fell across her shoulder like skeins of smoke. On her

deathbed she asked for crabapples. Tonight, my father burns
bamboo paper so my mother may have enough to eat.

How tender his fear that she could be hurt by a hunger
she can no longer feel. I watch him uncork his grief—tears

clinging to his cheeks like damp blossoms as he feeds the fire
that eats all that it touches. Over the burning pyre of ghost

money, my mother's dark hair rises and billows:
a cinch of smoke. A blindfold for the winter stars.

Gore Vidal Woke Up on Julian Assange's 52nd Birthday

| *JENNIFER MAIDEN*

(The *Security State* volume is Vidal's *History of the National Security State,* which Assange held as he was dragged from the Embassy.)

Gore Vidal woke up once more in Belmarsh Prison.
It was Julian Assange's fifty-second birthday and the cell
was like a china shelf of few but guarded possessions,
tea water, Vidal's own *Security State* volume,
chocolate biscuits, hi-res photographs of children
smiling in misty anxiety with their mother. All
the cards, letters, small souvenirs, supporters' mail
waited otherworldly in another room.
Vidal had felt dread at the request for all supporters
to post birthday greetings to Assange, their time
apparently no more use except for symbolism,
Assange's time too short except for consolation.
Vidal was braced for an America again
which was now he knew a bitter confused hell
where Russia and China alternated as demons,
the only freedom left a choice between them.
He said, 'I chose a house in Italy where the wail
from the sea was as sumptuous as Montaigne's
belief that truth was essential to conversation.
It is only for you I'd return where I was born.'
'Would I like to meet Montaigne?' asked Julian.
'Not yet. Not yet. Not yet. I don't think he is well
informed on Videos, Collateral Damage, Operation
Crazy Horse's namesake helicopter with the gun.
I'll parcel them up under "Truth" for him.
Of course it is good to have the truth in common.'
No doubt there were new things in the mail collection,
Julian, thought Vidal, could keep polished here as charms
but the *Security State* was not in as good condition
as when Assange gripped it from the Embassy in his arms.

Gorgon | ANDREW SUTHERLAND

for Finn O'Brainagain

i.

yesterday my shoulders seized up
exhaustion seeping past my eyes
I want to cry my body out of itself
into liquid. somehow preserve my
bone-dry hair, my gums.

this morning I thought I might tie my hair
in tiny knots, as if I were some lesser Björk,
but maybe all I'd be is scalp.

sing no words but keep a sound
find flow in sad-man demonstration
steady-cam the soft-snake gaze
make a path to the procession
act more to notice less.

ii.

off-weight always falling
walk skewing like a crab
zero core & all extremity
shake. then hug. locate
a mermaid-spine—rose
and banana to the base
before the drums begin—

iii.

this morning, when I lifted the blinds,
it felt like I was seeing the sun for the
first time in months. for a second, and
still maybe now, I felt I could be finally
ready to melt.

iv.

itching scratched into my hands,
my feet; the pus of some pimple
or some bite marking my kneecap
like a milk-white eye. at breakfast
I obsess over a matted knot in my
hair, while a man over the speakers
raps pussy, pussy, pussy. *can't*
believe it's only been two days,
says Michelle. sometimes you see
them glance away, avert their eyes,
turn to their partners like *what have*
you brought me to? but sometimes
one will plant their eyes to face you,
like: I know what this is. I see; go on.
go on, go on, gorgon, before I'm gone.

v.

at the aquarium today:
    all those jellyfish
    pufferfish, lionfish, stonefish
    degrees of pain for poison

an octopus stuck to the glass
a coiled sea snake, hidden face
a starfish in a child's hands

    nurse sharks
    the stingrays
    a sea turtle larger than any of them

and later at home:
    Uma Thurman
    Jolin Tsai
    a shot of Harry Hamlin

staring at reflected clay.

A Grass Tree by Any Other Name | LUKE PATTERSON

Flora and fauna have taken over the apartment.
We come together spreading like wild fire, like rain.
Not the Country we had hoped—three flights high
On stolen land—but it's our slow-growing peace
For when we tire of the Australiana Dreamtime.
A place we can hang our emu feather earrings,
Wash ochres from each other's skin, leave our keys
In a coolamon carved from the knee of a river red,
Without white superstition or political subtext.
Spectacles recede into the chirping suburban buzz
And flushed by an ancient patience, green thumb,
I watch your hedge magic season our landscape
In wetness opalescent as crocodile tears. Almost
Lyrical, the way you spin leaf and afternoon light.
A ceremony, taking your time tending the grass
Tree, potted knee-high, stump burnt black, stem
Sun-soaked and sprouting past our heads. Flowering
Names we keep secret. This bush love sacred.

I attend a private party several thousand times

that month. January 2023. It has three participants. Me,

Joseph Mount from Metronomy doing a DJ set in 2006 and my

spiritual guide, Post-Script.

Get on the course, I say to myself but I'm not sure where I stowed the

directions. The party begins in several time zones, not least chronological

and not more than… wait—forever.

Initiating trance, Post-Script whiteboards a gleaming treatise that we're all

grateful for and goes well with the sherbet beats and betas from Joe. Joe, why

so much grimace in *the Lab LDN sponsored by Smirnoff* vid? I recall the etymology of *post-script* from that moment

I looked it up in my *OED* (which I really have, I brought all volumes to the party) and share with the gang:

'1625 BACON *Ess., Cunning* (Arb.) 93, I knew one, that when he wrote a Letter, he would put that which was most Materiall, in the Post-script, as if it had been a By-matter.'[1]

Is the party the centre or the end, or does it pre-date my Materiall and my lust

for strife? What does the NME have to say on this. We google together, our three heads one

because *We Are Your Friends* (released by Justice, 3 July 2006 my birthday coincidence, non?) say P-S and J.

And they are. My friends. We cite musical differences for a while which are pleasant, vociferous

nothing to do with splits, all to do with collabs. And sweet, taut

remixes, right from the crowns of our supernova. Right from the guts of our wont.

1. Simpson, J. A. and E. S. C Weiner. *The Oxford English Dictionary.* 2nd ed. / Oxford : New York, Clarendon Press ; Oxford University Press, 1989.

Heyday | THEODORE ELL

You remember how the old home used to be.
Dry leaves matting the roof, loose doors, cobwebbed eaves.
Ready for doing up when we got round to it.

The fire-front took it like a hinge, back-broke it off.

To this day, there's only grass over brick-dust
and pitted cement. No sapling can go deep.
I don't hear many birds now or brush underfoot—

the new forest stands back in trained silences.

Chills, some mornings, and the scarp is still with me—
baked sandstone comes off like plates and pages now—
and I sometimes see slant shadows in the mist,

fixed bayonets. Warnings for the last to know.

As sunlight fills the chimney in the open
you see it holds our heyday, our beginnings
litter in the hearth. Spring has been torn from your years—

I nurse the next one, scattered, the soil my lifetime.

Hic Mulier | *KATE LILLEY*

1

She that hath pawned her credit to get a hat
will sell her smock to buy a feather.
She that hath given kisses to have her hair shorn
will give her honesty to have her upper parts
put into a French doublet.

2

Hyacinth, heliotropium, superfluous creatures.
A Masculine Woman makes the dew bitter.
Strange attire, hysteric afflictions,
a garment by day, a house by night.
Surely unseemliness is not too much to hope for.

3

The checkered pansy or particoloured heartsease
slips from her like tantalus fruit none can wear
but such as desire no more than they have.
So is she a Masculine Woman
that bereaves parents of authority, husbands of supremacy.

4

She that dare presume to overrule
although she neither paint, cut her hair
nor be deformed with new invented fashions
is notwithstanding
Hic Mulier.

5

She that spends more upon delicate cheer
or entertainment of a sweetheart in a month
than her husband may allow her for a year
          is *Hic Mulier*
whose tongue sets the world on fire
whose gestures, words, oaths betray her
          is *Hic Mulier*

Envoi

These women you hear brawling and scolding
have severally pissed on this bush of nettles
making the woman that waters them
as peevish for a day and as waspish
as if she had been stung in the brow with a hornet

Homebody | ELLA JEFFERY

Often we kicked it down at the cooldocks
where ships dragged in on coalish weather
and you'd get drunk, piss in the river.
Having nothing better to do I saw fit
to spend my life split:
embarrassment and ecstasy. It was easy,
then, being twenty. I didn't discern
my body's movement through time.
Now, having learned, I've turned back
to cities you shrugged off. Yes, you'd gloss this
as fear, my essential sin, and try to provoke
its twin, my rage. You'll never
move me again either way.

The Hourglass and the Pledge | ALEX SKOVRON

the ocean seldom repeats itself
—STANISŁAW LEM, *Solaris*

Or make that never. Channelling Herakleitos,
        I look up from the book: Nor does
a grain of sand, each one a crystal totally unique,
I remind myself (tautologies aside)—
        then hear myself elucidate a fresh conceit:
'An hourglass should possess a built-in bell':
to warn the watcher not to be distracted
        just as the stream accelerates
for the concluding grains to carve the rising cusp
to its destined geometry. Until the tables
        are turned … A new quote comes:
'The cost of flight is landing'—that's Harrison (Jim
not George), and the poet should know.
        Those specks of dust, trajecting in a quantum
beyond count, would have intrigued the atomists,
but Blake finessed the case. Not so the sea.
        It dances on its bed of sand, a skin concealing
a pledge never to reveal what it is thinking,
while its warning remains the same:
        Read in my undulations the fluid glass of time,
and dare to fathom the poem I never repeat.

i ain't reading all that / i'm happy for you tho / or sorry that happened

| *ALEX CREECE*

She owed us so many poems
—KEATON PATTI'S AI-BOT-INSPIRED OBITUARY
constructed one sentence per day

What if I don't have any poems left in me? Don't talk to me until I've had my cosmic comeuppance. It doesn't matter what happened to me in private; people will only ever remember that I was publicly insane. I used to love honey and fear drugs. Now I'm all drugs and bees, no sweetness. Perhaps I'm only human if you believe in me hard enough, if I'm sensible and sympathetic and ever so good. Enchanted by another snail, I weave desire paths through my own muck. Would I still make an iconic lollipop lady? Something something something fugue. In the emergency department, we are a series of questions without an appropriate checkbox. The waiting room full of false rainbows and unknown variables. My coming out story is the ballad of Earring Magic Ken. I don't want to perform wellness, but I don't want to perform sickness either. In your dreams, my mouth is Velcro, spilling scratchy secrets. In mine, my fears crumble to salt and I eat them on French fries. You untie my shoes for me when I'm too tired to put myself to bed. I don't notice until the next morning, when I'm moulding my feet back into shape. In the (psycho)tropics, nine out of ten GPs are frothing to shame my body for how it responds to antipsychotics. I recover from the eating disorder, and they breathe a sigh a relief that I am fodder for their fatphobia once more. I am diagnosed as a character from *Chicken Run.* I am both the nerd and the ditz in *Chicken Run.* I am the utopic lesbian aspirations of *Chicken Run.* The world is full of scheming plasticine rats, just like *Chicken Run.* I'm in love with the shape of *Chicken Run.* What does it mean when you get the Tuesday Suicides every day? I masturbate: is that a little suicide? I make a nest from my own hair because I don't trust anyone else's. I am a private menace, disturbing my own peace. All I want is to dilly dally. Too much dilly, not enough dally. Or vice versa. A dilly dally dilemma. I wish I could stifle the sound of my chaos into the tune of *The L Word* theme song. A different song plays. It's the music from reality TV dating shows that indicates a contestant is an utter clown. I don't want to kill a fly for buzzing. I don't want to destroy something simply because it's annoying. January melts and mumbles. Sorry for setting off your uncanny valley detector. Does this valley have a campground? My dad tells me of when his family home burned down around him, but he refused to leave until someone made him a ketchup sandwich. It's this, more than the shape of our elbows, that convinces me of genetics. I'm one minor inconvenience away from becoming a cartoon supervillain. I name my absent children after the noises in the attic, and all words lose their meaning. They call it semantic satiation. I fill in the blanks with lorem ipsum. Under this roof, we go off impulse. I'm addicted to competition shows where the judges cry a lot. I watch Insta videos of some guy eating porridge while covered in rodents. Frisson itches. You go away for a week, and I forget to nurture the parts of myself that make me a person. I let a spider claim the kitchen. The dog claims the bedroom, the cat claims my skin. I've never once felt refreshed in my life. Standing around like a person emoji, I fixate on hyperdontia. Hyperdontia wish your girlfriend had teeth like me. I want to be angry so badly, a pre-emptively clenched fist. My fursona is the dust monster from *Round the Twist.* It's easier to live in corners. Each cluster of breath tastes like a mistake, a sunflower smoke. Are these pareidolic faces mad at me? I am Zac Efron's pond reflection in the 'Bet On It' number in *High School Musical 2* – a shittily edited facsimile of a star. All lesbians are jellicles, but craving oat milk instead of rebirth. At a social function, I tell someone's grandpa that I'm a tooth-eating dentist to conceal my identity as a tooth-wearing poet. Is it so wrong to write? Less of a river, more of a sludge-covered rock jammed in its craw. My assailant is now someone's husband; I'm wed only to my willpower. He's the apple of her eye, but he squirms at my core, a toxic gut full of worms, soured. I'm the bridegroom of sweet revenge, cold revenge, of revenge for the ragamuffin, rascal, rapscallion, rat bastard. There's a bunion bioluminescent on the cusp of my life. I'm ripping out the tags and cosplaying in your old clothes. In queer company, and only here, I'm suddenly feminine. I was always the boy in the playground, the honorary husband, frog, or piece of furniture, if I was ever permitted to play at all. I'm a disaster of a girl, but I refuse to be anything else. Mrs. Jingles died today. I spent my first day of school playing hide-and-seek, with no one coming to find me. I don't own an accurately functioning clock, not even the *Shrek* one. Time skips. I step out of this poem for a few days. I'm more flexible than people think, contorting into yoga poses in the liminal space, packing myself up like a saggy old mattress, drenched in campfire beans. There's an apricity to my burnout on a crisp morning, curling my singed edges. If life were an urban legend, I'd be a mere gerbil and the world would be Richard Gere's butt. All my targeted ads describe themselves as 'buttersoft', and I develop a Pavlovian response to my non-dairy margarine alternative spread. I doomscroll too hard, entering a dimension where my least favourite person lip-synchs my least favourite song (and they're not even a drag queen). At dawn, I walk past all the rich houses in a neighbouring suburb, their silence like a status symbol. I pick my wedgie as I pass the fanciest mansion. I am the Garfield of this very moment. Every alien abduction story is weirdly horny; I just want extra-terrestrial kinship. I rejuvenate my line readings, soap-scummed and palms pruning. We load up on discount vegetables, but you're the only one who envisions what they can become. Alone, I puff up spores. I'm that person buying the trendy flavours of classic products – Oreos, crisps. Is it my fault there's Vegemite everything? The world's greatest poem is whatever is going through my dog's mind when she nibbles on my fingernail. I can't compete with that, but why are we always competing? Maybe this is enough, whatever it is. Scream-happy in a Spotlight store, I stifle conspiracy theories about their ugly, bland fabrics. I morph into a nightmare femme on the floor of a Bunnings, bleeding glitter glue. I saw a turtle today, but there were already two people with nose rings taking pictures of it, and I didn't want to make it three of us. A villain, or cat from *Cats* the musical, says 'I am'. A hero, or a poet, says 'I want'. But I am what I want, and I want to be a poetic cat. The teddy bear on the side of the road destroys me with a siren song. Each day is an heirloom fruit. I never learnt to play chess. I fill my time with rodent funerals, spacing out beneath an uninvited daytime moon. I lived with someone for four years without ever knowing the scrawl of her handwriting. I want to plant enough trees to offset my existence. This sounds like shit when Siri reads it. Does it sound any better in my voice? In your head? Why must I always wait to be emboldened, struck by lightning, before I can say a word? Poetry is so fucking embarrassing.

they said… we are the dust that fine-silts your skin   we are brown
rivers   blue oceans   pink lakes   purple skies   we are fresh water
salted   mined / cracked / drilled   we agitate and distil with mud and
clay   then we rise   awake in the wake   afloat on a legacy that churns
into trouble   and we refuse to be left behind.

they said… we are your constant   we cast shadows and secrets to wax
and wane   caress your face so you glow   we will lure you in and tug
at your heart   we will bathe you   sedate you   shine through night so
you grow toward the sun.

they said… we will surprise you with our velocity   suck the air from
your lungs and whip through your hair so your dark eyes sting   inhale
slowly   with focus   see your flesh tremble   we will teach you to fly
to the stars   this vast complex intricate web of night   there is so
much to say here and we promise to point you home.

they said… bend and glide and carve your way back   this is your journey
to meet the sea   currents will pull you under   for this freshwater spirit
has much to share   you will be gifted gills to breathe in the deep   you
will erode silt barriers   welcome the flow   there will be no
horizons when you arrive   so hold space for the immensity as we siren-
call you   cradle and rock you   we will not let you go.

they said… plant these seeds   grow story-trees with deep roots and life-
giving canopies to shelter and nourish and bloom   remember to lean
in close   recognise the colour of survival   what it looks / feels /
tastes like   we will haunt you and make noise   for the air that you
breathe   for clean water you need   for the skin that you bear   for
the right to flow free   for the lovers you choose   for love of
Country   and do not worry   time can't erode your spirit or your
place   know that you belong.

they said… seek us in rainbows and fractures of light   we will find
you   drink nectar from your lips and salt from your tongue   introduce
you to yesterday's breeze   and soar into tomorrow   everywhere
afloat   impossible to contain.

After the summer burn this rain so light
it evaporates before hitting the ground.
But summer isn't over and far across the continent
rain is falling so long and hard that ground
is immiscible with shapes that will never reform
in the same way. To travel incognito is to abbreviate
part of the self to meet conditions as you imagine
them, or as they might be. Subterfuge or safety?
At a time when travel is inhibited, your incognito
is like living as so many others are dying.

I can't speak of the places I've been when the sky
is turning shades of blue and gray, is fulminated red
or coping with breath of rockets in all their
deployments. How can a book end when there are
others being written, and in this fact you sign
your hope: a signature you've forgotten but scrolls
automatically. How glib is the Doppler radar?
The rituals I've resolved are those for preserving
the house—not against but out of calibration
with ants, mice and rabbits. The inner outer thing.

I diminish my vocabulary to expand my understanding
of these experiences of static and stillness.
A prognosis of native blue-banded bees which
have seemed absent from usual places this year.
A psychoanalysis of absence. A dereliction of cause,
a tribulation of effect. 'Doomscrolling' events into ellipses,
that state as opposed to graves that are memory.
How we hear the galloping disaster. How we tune in
and out. Our jump-cut vision. What we conceal and what
we know. No franchise, no spoils, but new notes for return flight.

It always starts the same

early tides turning
gaps at the bottom of the world
.`'`.`.'`'`.~.`'~.`'`.
a celestial dome settles
vast biomes
a baby moon
all of nature thinking
=-=-_-_=_-=_=_=-==-=-_-_=_-=_=_=-==-=-_-_=_-=_-
breathless ponds
,.,.,.
hollow depths
.,,-,,...._.--...--+--.,,-,.-
-.,_,.-=~'`^`'~=-.,_,.-=~'`^`'~=-.,.-=~'`^`'~=-.,_,
half-remembered fossils
.,,-,,...._.--...--+--.,,-,.-
an unconnected world
.~"~._.~"~._.~"~.
deliberate elevations
infinite generation
.,,-,,...._.--...--+--.,,-,.-
tender aquifers
potential monoliths
coarse bodies
corporeal intrusions
~~~~~~~~~ ~~~~~~~
make perlin worms
smooth rough edges
scale new layers
precious clay
hidden sussurations
veins forming
a cold dawn
.`'`.`.'`'`.~.`'~.`'`.

Scan QR code to view the digital version of this poem on *The Suburban Review*'s website, where readers can generate different iterations of this poem.
~~~~~~~~~

bureau says the sun just smoked my best incense
the sparkly stuff come from my soft past
red dirt spreads *very quickly*
happens to be my *street-directory*
are you waiting for potential eat

potential *energy*
of cheese losing grip
open that industrial pineapple scroll waiting there in napkins like a statue
designed and erected stale to last the entire hungry era
i am done with transition filled my bag with biological pick n mix
now i'm donating incense to the stealth
my 9 spare-lives
b o b b i n g along the conveyer belt

donating incense to the closed curtains
dusting closeted adolescence with pollen
like propagate
like relief is a sacred totem
pass it round the class
let everyone touch it
smudge it, spread it
if that's what it takes
to push-back against
parents relax -at the end of
the day-
gender is no accident
cheese sizzling, slippery shoulder
hubcap silver

The good news about the end of days is
you've got something to write about.
The bad news is. Don't let that deter you.

There are 1000 films to see before you die
and some of them are ten hours long
and some of them you can't buy.

Invite the shifty duo from the Sleven
back to Benji's for kick-ons. Krank
the stezza Samantha Sang sings:
'Cry me a river that leads to your ocean.'

There'll be nobody left in this world.
Don't despair. Go full 80s: metal hair,
Apple IIes and Corey Haim, ozone holes and
acid rain. Summer love is not the same.

Little Heartbeats | JILL JONES

I don't know anything
about blue &
gusts play around birds

Jasmine these days
is a co
incidence

Obstinacy—red
as summer's
dirty secret

Hair keeps growing &
I float
in tide

•

My nerves—
threading windows
Give me the map!

The browsing cure-all
only covers
so much

I wonder what is
length & rain
is deeper in afternoon

Should I
gush all the love &
stop frowning

•

Help me Venus!
I know you're up there
in the busy stars

A luxuriant gamble—
the dictionary at 3am
into the yellow yonder

I'm working
on the fly as a
friend of night

Three words watch me—
book, bowl, window
above any purpose

The closest I've ever come to an iceberg is at the bottom of a dime bag. Me, a climate of catastrophe, aching for the melt. Apply barrel butt to crush chemical into sliver and shard. Soak, watch landscape become liquid. There were nights when I was so far spun that room wouldn't stop spinning and, for comfort, I would play the sound of Antarctica's icebergs succumbing to the heat. Scree and sheets tearing apart. The melody epic in the magnitude of one form embracing another to become. Salt song, undoing. One time, in the throes of psychosis, as this serenade filled the room, I imagined my extremities populated by penguins. An itch of flippers. Cacophony of beaked throng. Gay couples hatching eggs. The pull into an imagined micro: my body became lynchpin of a southern pole. Huge heaving hull, frozen. Teeth the mass beneath, grinding. Eons in the space of unravelling. I believed myself fluent in flightless tongue. When I came down, my body was a puddle in the middle of a wrecked mattress. Below the ice is the rubble of rock, clinging to what it once was.

plummeting   / south
through   a rocky
amphitheatre   browns
and creams   specked
purple   and red /
cut   at /
differing   an   \   \   gles
/   \ reminiscent   of Richter’s
/   \   *Abstrakt*   /   \ *Bilden*
cross   hatched   in cracks   /
/ a sandstone   canvas
pierced   by oaks /   mist in   the branches /
in distance /   in   time \   in the clouds it takes
for distance   to disperse   / shroud   \   \
\   you in rain /   at the
\   centre   / of   some   interstice
waiting   for paint   to dry   atop
a   question /
or to turn   and /   away
from this   lock / the i   dea of   no \
thing   between   glass /
to scratch   /   to smear   / but not   cut
\ \   /   the heart
\   from body   \ \ \   ’s canvas
/   in the always   seeking /   always   the me
aning   of   which   a foot   print /
\   a breath   / carbon   as a   measurement
/   of simplicity \   com   plicity
\ \   / land   scape   as image
the *je pense*   \ *donc*   *je suis*   almighty
hierarchy   \ of   interpretation   gob

smacked   at   the sight /   the site \
of   machines   that cut \   this   rock
/ that   tarred   this place /
this winter   morning   warm   earl   grey
driving   across   /
expanse's   undulation \   \ \
where   \   / /   \
t   /   stand like   \
e /   \   conquistadors   /
l   in an imperialistic   \
e \   house /   and in   that sense
g p   / /   how /   define   a / canvas
r o \   \ if not   hands   dragging
a l   brushes   / across   history's
p e   /   cra /   cked   highway
h s   or that   billboard   / /
/   outside \   Heathcote
returning   like   \ a refrain

This is Dharawal Country
Drive Safe

MIDWINTER DAY | KEN BOLTON

off to pick up Noah

a lift?   No

I walk, hands in pockets, shoulders hunched

        in the sun

        made to feel   like James Dean
                              in a famous picture

                consequently, handsomer, too
                                        tho I don't imagine
I really am

I'm whistling
                    a tune I whistle a lot

                    tho what is it exactly

                early Wayne Shorter

I say hullo to an old lady coming my way
                    80 maybe

then what was I thinking about? —

        of *Midwinter Day* ?

                                        I read it in 1982

imported direct from Small Press Distribution

tall & blue—dark blue—& the format a little big
so I have always to find a place for it
or forget
—search—
& think, "Must've lent it to someone"
— "And I know
just whom."
Then months later see it again
or 'years later' it seems

had I given it to Ann
in a fit of niceness
self-renunciation?
Not me,
as it turns out
There it is. Have I ever

actually, finished it?

I know the first pages well,
but I
have
no memory of its end

Bits of Alice's podcast
make it seem unfamiliar

So maybe not.

Up on the main road, across from the school
it's mostly guys—usually plenty of mums—to
pick up the kids

who mass soon, at the lights
in small groups of twenty or so—on foot, on
bikes—& a mum or dad or two between. Noah
is always in the third batch.

The tune is
'Moon of Manakoora'

I walk a street or two & turn, where the new place is going up
enormous slab, piles & racks of wood, ready, waiting, ready to go

then up Cumberland beside the oval to the main road, & left
to the traffic lights—offered a lift by another parent starting out
but I prefer to walk

#

as I said, unaccountably jaunty

— (the song) —

tho no red jacket
or Jimmy's face so photogenic

#

Turns out I don't know the beginning either—
but the section further on where she talks about
people, the others all about her, I know.

And later there's that good patch
where she lists everything—every thing
she does, incidents, chores, difficulties,
interruptions—memories—then every business or building
in the small American town, a tour.

Large parts of the poem are on target
Larger parts are not. The dreams, the default
reliance on beads & feathers & mythology
that isn't hers. *Midwinter Day* makes its point,
signals its type well—but muffs the execution.
Making Mayer exemplary as an experimentalist,
she proves her point: '*This* could be done.'
but not such a good poet: large parts are dull—
the standard American regard for dreams and
analysis—as in "Georgette's analyst says…" —to
no real end. Almost like superstition. The archetypes.

"Hullo, Noah. How was it today?"

My Kathy Acker | ABBRA KOTLARCZYK

(Corymbia citriodora)

I'm by the Lake
reading Jackie Wang's
grieving turn away from
another body of water when I
cross the bridge turn away from
this collection
of spent vessels still
coursing while a black
swan aerates its middle down
stream. I leave the swan red mouth-

ed into its host
body and walk up the
hill to visit My Kathy Acker.
There are a few around the neigh-
bourhood but this is the original and
the best. She is a
french bulldog in stat-
ure relative to nearby tower-
ing standards and smooth all
muscle body been building here

for quite some time
adjacent to this
forever time waterway.
She stands in perpetual stre-
tch one dominant limb—a trunk
—away from the
body of the Lake as if
a missive poised above her head.
My Kathy Acker could make
me a tree hugger yet. She is glorious

strong with
smooth weather-
ed skin pastel pinks
and blues scribbly veins
indicative of the presence of
a uterus—but we
won't get into essentials
—they preamble up the vent-
ricle vertical non-stretching arm
pockmarks down her northern most side.

She is the living
embodiment of pres-
ervation of erosion. My
own private Kathy Acker is
a limb-loosener when the breeze

fondles gently her lanc-
eolate leaves island oil glands sweating lemon-scented
semes corpuscular into
mass bulging as when freshly baked
bread escapes the score line. A whole matrix of

her lattice in the attic
of this matriarch—but we
won't get into essentials—each
bulge a conjunction to the built en-
vironment. *If, but, and…* I cross her and

observe the breakdown of language
all
at angles.

How to reconcile the
            fact of this glory
as a failing?

My Kathy Acker is not
mine and I repeat
this mantra to
myself
            daily.

My TED Talk: | OUYANG YU

You have to do it badly. If it is poetry, even more so, because there is no because. If you write like you were the best in the world, you are the worst because you pretend too hard. Too harsh, too. Why do you want to be the best? Is that because you are a lack or there is a lack in you that you feel like filling up all the time? Even when you are named the best, does that mean anything? What about those who are not named the best? What about those who are not even called the good? Do we have to be good in order to survive? Survive what? But poetry is freedom. It frees you from all the constraints, restraints and limitations of the world because of good, better, best. It doesn't work like that in poetry. When you tell yourself to write the best poem in the world now, you will not get anywhere. You won't even produce a single line. Best is the symbol of the worst oppression and suppression. It stops you from even producing the mediocrest work. Why don't you say to yourself: I'm not good enough. I'm already bad. From time to time, I feel I have no abilities to do anything well. I am stifled by the competition around me. Everyone is pushed to a choking level. I don't want to be a president, not even of a company, not even a class, let alone a country. All I ever want to do is a poet. And a bad poet at that. Why? I mean who can be *that* good without making a huge effort? And the point? Nothing guarantees that you won't die. In fact everything guarantees that you do. I write without knowing what I write is good or bad. I write without wanting to know. Anything and everything are subject to judgement by other people anyway. Who has the autonomy to do what one likes to the ultimate degree of pleasing oneself? Why does one imprison oneself with the concepts, ideas, ideologies, judgments and confinements of other people? Aren't there too many prisons already in this world? To be bad is to be free. To be bad is to be creative. To be bad is to be innovative. Marcel Duchamp is bad because he buys a readymade and presents it as art in a museum. Piero Manzoni is bad because he cans his own shit and sells it for millions of dollars after his death. Andres Serrano is bad because he makes 'Piss

Christ.' Michael Jackson is bad because he makes an album titled, *Bad*. Maurizio Cattelan is bad because he creates 'Comedian' out of a duck-taped banana. Banksy is bad because he self-destructs his own art. Ouyang Yu is bad because he writes a poem called 'Bad Writing'. All histories are a continuous process of badness against goodness until it becomes good then badded again. It's a process of keep saying 'my bad', 'our bad', 'their bad'. I love bad. There's nothing else I love. I only love bad. Let the good rot for all I care.

1 March 1916— wax poetical a magnificent
night with crystal clear atmosphere the moon
almost on horizon resembles the golden horn
of fairy tales pending in a lustrous firmament
bespangled with brilliants & one's imagination
running riot might conjecture a blast sounded
on horn will break the magic of this sight as
moon dips & faint orange blush suffuses its
path which broadens & glows til dawn spreads
with tints of pink & blue & the dissipation of
night's enchantment discloses immense pools
of still water surrounding our island floe from
which clouds of frost smoke lazily arise golden
in the rising Sun the beau ideal of our dreams

No Picnic! | PETE SPENCE

Everybody has got something to
hide except me and my lobster

everyone seems to be eager for lunch
but it hasn't arrived yet and there's
no sign of its approach even the clouds
seem weak with hunger the empty
plates echo off walls has the World
Catering Authority flown the coop?
Caviar Emptor! no blancmange only blank
menus! the painters lay down their brushes
and come in from the desert somewhere
a radio is playing **Rock Lobster!**

1. Nothing

At a certain density anything
becomes a black hole. Lighthouse. Line. Schwarzschild
radius of a mother. Which is to
say black hole and lighthouse are selfsame, down
to the matter of measurement, and the
arrangement of particles that renders
me daughter is lineage heavier
than singularity. Let's say black holes
are messengers, let's say the gap between
ancestor and inheritor is the
broken line forcing a poem to hang
on the possibility of all things
in vibrating superposition, un-
til collapsing under the weight of sight.

2. Nowhere

The problem with a point of no return
is teleological in nature.
One must know the spectrum of future space
-time to determine when light can only
pass inward, or where too much is enough.
A mother says 'sorry, what did you say?'
and a daughter, out of time, replies (
)—knowing a black hole is a
lighthouse is a daughter is that with an
empty (   ) space at its centre, and
were a mother to send a daughter past
an event horizon, she would never
appear to cross it. Floating in free fall,
the last courier runs from the old world.

3. At Some Point

In the telescope glints a galaxy
four point six billion years past (extinct), so
it stands to reason some future prophet
—disappointed, like all daughters, by all
politics of her nation—peers down to
watch us now through her great eye, then, growing
bored, dictates to her Google Doc (forgive
my lack of imagination) that the
temperature of this earth's core and its
largest star were remarkably close, at
five thousand, two hundred and five thousand,
seven hundred and seventy-eight—give
or take world's end—degrees Celsius, so
'that must have meant something,' she says. 'It must.'

Passing Through Chicago | PETRA WHITE

Rivers of road, rivers of river, snow-clumped trees,
the angel, flowering in moonlight.
People would have muttered if they'd seen.
What good is an angel now?
His terrifying beauty, hidden beneath a wing.
If we think we could be rescued
from the fate we've shored up,
it is not an angel, it's a person, rising out of flames.
Perhaps the angel, fallen to earth as lightly
as a feather from a falcon, has nothing to offer but himself,
pale clawed feet in the dark street, his feeble torch
on this avenue of twitching flags, threads of a great anxiety.
He crawls into the attic of number 1813.
In the space between home and state,
the angel shudders, turns, cramped wings shake open—
through the house a molten dream, through breakfast and dinner,
through the silver sorrows of the city,
its lumpy cracked streets, its America, soaring in the snow.

The Pazzi Conspiracy Medal: Giuliano Murdered *Reverse:* Lorenzo Escapes The Assassins

LISA GORTON

That afternoon *Il Magnifico* stood in the window of his palace, a bandage at his throat, clothes stained with blood—said, 'Do not harm the innocent'—They had thrown the conspirators from the high windows of the Signoria—left them to hang—the mercenaries they killed inside the building—bodies stripped naked, hacked apart—now a head fixed on a spear—torso on a sword-tip—to be carried through the streets—'so many deaths that the streets were filled with the parts of men'—dead bodies propped inside the windows of the notaries—'naked as the day they were born'—and they looked 'like men created to look alive'—like those effigies Verrocchio made with Orsino the waxworker—skeletons of wood bodied with woven reed—flesh of waxed cloth, folded—head, hands and feet of wax cast from life and painted wet on wet—'so life-like that they seemed no images in wax but living men'—and one they dressed in the blood-stained clothes that *Il Magnifico* wore that day—propped by the miraculous crucifix of the Chiarita where once San Zanobi healed a rich man of his sore throat—and one they dressed in his *lucco,* inside the door of *Santa Annunziata,* kneeling by the place where candles are sold—its bodies on horseback, bodies in armour, bodies strung from ropes—its hands of wax and eyes, ears, teeth, arms—and chains of silver—chains of iron—brides came to leave their flowers there where once an angel painted the virgin's likeness while a painter slept in despair of imagining the beauty of her face—and they paid Orsino the waxworker twelve fiorini—and the two boy choristers in the train of Cardinal Riario, crossing the square to the palace, were torn apart by the crowd—

Faceless profiles confess that they find my body desirable.
They say how my skin 'glows!'
Indeed it radiates faster than my wit can come to terms with our…
'Meet up'
arrangement.
I'm curious as to where this stranger can lead me through some
curvature of my own body,
I myself do not know the whereabouts to
See in personless love,
it removes the fear of attachment,
because I can't love someone without a heart.
But I can love the person they see me to be
for in that spare moment,
I'm purpose without a journey
Because we've already arrived.
They're finished,
they're done for the night,
until they need their next hit of brief love to sustain themselves,
sustaining by performance,
selling a show abandoned by their bedded truths.
While masquerading their lies that they never loved this body.

Poesy | *AUTUMN ROYAL*

When people speak out in favor of a life of madness, they mean the cute, nice madness, not the disgusting or dangerous kind. The disgusting and dangerous kind is prioritized in language but not in life.
—AASE BERG

The dash between shelf and life—why do you think I chose you?
I'm a cornice, a decorated projection at the heights of desire—
disenchanted and plastered for the sake of the walls. I'm off
chops at a speed before murder was just a concept—it only takes
a few minutes. I'm attached to the top floor yet down pitched
as I mark virtue. I mark from a hospital bed—they strapped
and pressed me as to why I needed care—in the car, in the kitchen,
in the office chair. They question why I hugged the shaking man
after the meeting—I beg them. I hoard. I'm a version of editing
archetypes and questioning why I'll never be an inborn model.
I opinion—*I* but hope to mean *we* while the death poet becomes
me as I pump petrol into my car, my vehicle—my mouthpiece.
I lie down on a couch and complain about not having a couch—
yet I promised to be static—happy to live in the shed knowing
it's further than what's expected. I'm threatening with my passivity,
dissolving fizz—formerly still *now*. The crudeness of a rubric—
I mark essays, I mark essays, I mark essays. I mark. I am a mark.
I am marked with deadlines. I mark a high distinction when all
I need is credit—feedback with no response and just for beads—
Trying to investigate meaning and watering soil with spite.
It only takes a few minutes for the organs, the mud, and handlings
of conversations about the sours of milk—found, smelt and drunk.

we're post glitch

OK

a breeze moves through the server

OK

and living lowered binary against ancestral

OK

we're post glitch

OK

of the digital native born

OK

and you already know this is deliberate
OK
that began when the digital frontier went live
OK
placed basket on data upstream
OK
hear the true languages coded on the tongues
OK

Scan QR code to view the interactive digital version of this poem on *crawlspace*'s website.

There's no separating it
in this world nor the next.
        Evil is granular and supple.
The gritty blood under fingertips
is full of it as much as the victim's
organs slapped on the sand
by this river where
Death is the instrument of pines.
        Plastic is obligatory for evildoers.
You can keep things in it without spilling.
You can get it anywhere. It scrubs up nice.
Then, when you're done, there's a package
for the unwrappers to raven through.

        1. The cat on the bed whirrs like a fur heart.
My head pyramid is looted by a death cult:
they deal the darts of the dodo dance.
        2. Evil is the shadows on the wall of the cave:
you dress your daughter as a giant eyeball
then shove a mike in her gaping pupil.

Do what you love
        I'd do it
Fuck what you love
        I'd fuck it
All doing
        Is a death ray
                To fuck the one you love.

Up, up, my friends! — to the lodge, to the dark
wood and eyebrows over sherry
incest and dwarves and rot-slickened teens,
old tech, corkscrew perms, '90s drugs,
demonic frost crystals choking the ash brook,
fern and dale lynched by the forking horn,
every rope recoiled down its own throat
and, for you, friends, your fingers thrust in the fire
till your skin and muscle melt
like the wickedest Witch of the West
and the tumbling knucklebones rattle
in the white-hot grate — don't think
I won't come for you through the mirror
lapping at your terror like a starving kitten milk.

Prospect Park | GARETH MORGAN

the banana tastes like petrochemicals
i'm chiquitita in the dog park, pink sea
of humans and dogs

i guess i could have said it seems
like you have a lot of nice friends
rather than explaining my foreignness again

a red bird foraging for my
chemically banana—the light is dusky
but warmed up enough to sit

there are many kinds of sugar on this planet
ludic sock puppet—what sock puppets aren't?
dog people are dull well not all dog people

but this lady who left her treat bag at home
so Bell is feeling deprived—poor Bell...

i part the green sea with my helmet firmly on
and on the hill i climb another hill

Pulp to reform | PAM BROWN

this is
    my first interview
        since my death

(predictable suspense)

        i swallowed
        a cotton bud

i had only just
recovered
from the teardrop curse

by then
it had become popular
    to pulp to reform

everyone's dad
            shredded
their rhetorical filler

that seemed to work
for them
            the dads

every one of them
    had sampled
a few mls of
ostensibly beneficial
            dribble

copper bracelets
    were big too
&
    old brass bowlfuls
of plant-based plants

- - -

some perspective
in the kitchen –

rinsing
        greasy glass lids
            foam bubbles

little transparent
      purplish white globes
          slide   ping   pop

cartoon
georges perec
      moments

like
question your teaspoons
(questionner tes petites cuillèrs)

drumming
        steel cutlery
    to set the table

i asked
the pot plant
    what to do

begin straightaway
                        cook up
easy parasite stir fry

that's what
the dads
called it

unwelcome comments

--- --- --- --- ---

out in the street
on the odd numbers side
                a house number
                            is missing

heading
north to south
       facing east

into sunrises
pinkish or reddish
on a good morning

this is 147
the hermit's at 149

151 is missing
no house no number
then
the rental terrace 153

day breaks
over the flitting zone

wind drops
its
sootsoaked aerosols

swallows chit chit
                    to the clouds –
'you're across everything'

dreamliner
slices cirrus vapour

morning's daze
            crashed
by an airwave nail gun

pump pat
pump pat
pump pat

loud ricochet
swooshes off the fence

--- --- --- --- ---

before
i died

i had
to get away

crosshatched
nerves twitched

i deserved
a different body
smooth & calm
 &
    maybe lanky

- - -

i was
always polite
     &
       friendly

at the clinic
at the deli
at the library

at the fish shop

'kalispera
          tikanis?'

my few greek expressions
had come from
a worldly lesbian
who'd been to samos

she'd learned them
from her ouzo lover
('s'agapo poli')
or
was it retsina?

'efcharistó
télos pánton'

i should have
gone
to samos

thanks
anyway

--- --- --- --- ---

this interview
has digressed

i'm not sure
what you want
to know

is it
about the poetry?

all
    accidental

from this cardboard coffin
            some final words –

Note: Pulp was an English art pop band in the mid 1990s. In late 2022 the poet Michael Farrell posted their news on Facebook using the headline 'Pulp to reform'.

Michael posted '"Pulp to reform" sounds like a pam brown poem title.'

So I wrote a poem that really had nothing to do with the band but later, as poetry often does, its content took on a synchronistic cast of mortality. Pulp were due to reform in 2023, but, sadly, in early March the bass player, Steve Mackey, died.

Reality | S. K. KELEN

Reality bends into itself, we think we're going places
but the highway we travel is a Möbius strip.
Allies bomb civilians in far-off lands
to free them: Irony is a grim killer.
There must always be enemies employed,
deployed and supplied by the military industry—
they are targeted, destroyed and are replaced, supplied
then targeted. Our times are a dark story unfolding like an epilogue
for *1984*, a novel by George Orwell (published in 1949) or
a final scene, overseas, the actors in a crazy *Star Wars*
episode written on a CIA storyboard, the agents have paradise
treasure in their eyes, monumental flames lick the sky.
Fight the latest menace. Safe home: relieved viewers
watch the tragicomedy with green-screen eyes.

Relevant to the Day | OMAR SAKR

The story of a murder crosses the globe
in a heartbeat or breath
and people everywhere are talking.
The act of dying opens so many chests.
Outside, Poe stares at me from within a raven
so I shout, 'Remove yourself, stupid man!'
Due to what I have read, every black bird
is weighed down by a sickly sad man.
How depressing. I shake the image into a caw,
tree tops, an unsolvable mystery.
Anyway, people are grieving a music lost,
and I listen as they fall deeper into themselves.
The Venn diagram of those who believe
love at first sight is a myth & people who weep
the instant they learn of a loved one passing
is a perfect circle—how knowledge enters
the body and when it leaves are the concerns
of those most determined to make
their own meaning. By coincidence,
it is they who wind up faithless, alone
with their hands and chance. The Arctic is melting,
a phrase I do not understand. Can anyone?
To stand under means 'to be close to'
and we cannot be close to what vanishes,
which is the world, or at least the parts I live on
and that I must admit I enjoy. Here, to vanish is
to become unfamiliar, hostile, strange—a polar bear
in Aldi, a headless galloping, a name unending.

would you rather a day off
or a loyalty rewards card? used to be
you had a cubicle of your own, used to be
you could shake hands with almost anybody—
today I'm back to scarecrow duty, failing upwards.
could this have been an email? am I maximising
my solidarity here? it's wise to keep a few tricky
secrets between you and the boss, it shows
you're one to be trusted, living punk rock on an Arts
budget. they'll offer it as an opportunity, not a
favour, that's what management is now, we
learnt it in a workshop. we never tell, we suggest
and follow up. just remember that they're reading
your emails, and cache is the enemy, always.
would you rather time in lieu or overtime?
we've being quietly reinventing the way
brands like yours own the checkout process,
king of the buy now pay later, I skate through the
CRM like Prince Albert, Coburg bound.

The Resurrection of the Body as Zombie Movie

| *JOSIE/JOCELYN SUZANNE*

We watch them, evening coffees miraculously
clasped, still. They walk, not shamble, just
as normal, thirty to a mass, dressed
for work. When they gaze upon us, stock
still on our porches, house timber wholly ecosystem
of termites, petitioning the moon
to reappear each night, holding time, they look
only, stitched. You imagine they're wearing
make-up. They are, but not to convey
anything. This is only how they present. You observe
your gran moving, a body rent, slightly
faster than she used to. A few absent-mindedly
pushing her along, a few fingers on her
elbow, her spine. The moon is clearer than any leaf
in the street-puddles, reaching to storm-drains
along the curbs: you could map
each lunar volcano, each *maria* containing still
water— you picture— the topography
of empty basins. The stragglers walk down the curb
into the bush. You're listening to the song
"Hebrews 11:40" by acclaimed dad-rock band
The Mountain Goats, sing "*itches hiding in
the brambles*", you mishear. You picture
the word "witch" detaching themselves from their
referent, growing wings, mandibles, a departure of eyes
you watch them disassemble, returning
wherever they came— still— in the meteoric air.

Dear Runbatty:
Everybody in the end's gaing Crackdown Natty.
Hallucinated flames
        In place of Deloraine Cathedral
The night at least as sweet and certain as a death-pact in a harem
Havin' a noggin built for headbuttin'
                                        and rare thought
Your hair I find is finer in design than Lucifer's wallpaper

A sort of serious haze that is still wildly amateurish
One of those select Tipperary Warblers who prefer pissing *en plein air*
All my knickers knackered in their elastic a sort of historical freedom
I don't hate the world but I do want an elaborate personal apology from
The Galway Masochists
    Institute of Treachery's
        Doctor Orla Flynn

Which I did just now receive: 'You can do whatever you want Doogal
        including drop dead'
A pretty masterpiece of personal gripedom
"& please return your overdue nymphs to the Institute's carnal collection
Theyre here somewhere I fear
        Near the fat pamphlet of 'the terrible changeable moods of the
        Beloved' left out deliberate in the rain

Hello bright spot of Angel Light that crosses my eyes some times
Prettiest girl than never I saw an her name was Douglass-Mary
        (Feckless Mary)
Whose beauty was first touched upon in the pages of 'The Flaming
        Dickhead Review'

A'hm going out to purchase a Sheepskin coverlet
For my Wang dang ding-along dinga-linga
wing-dang
do
to feel more of the 'pagan-fancy'
'it's got sublime all over it!!!!!'

Whats your current obsession? Eileen: 'Polyamoury'
What about your polyamourees? Eileen: 'Carnage'
At which point we say good on you Eileen

'I feel like women would be more ruthless in war than men!'
Good on *you* Sophie
Youre the cutest little underbug I ever did see
Now what is the name of the current Termite King?
The Rage
The Rage
More lastingly lamentable than a blackhole named after your ma
Folk tales of folk terror
Now with added accurate data fallen star son of perdition
Ruler of this world
& lonelier than a Stalingrad cowboy dancing to techno in a St. Petersburg carpark
Happier than a St. Petersburg cowboy dancing to techno in a Stalingrad fairground
The thistlemilkers the venom elect
I'd like a poem that works as a charm
Built like a trilling of rattlesnake peptides
Emollient to embalm
Kill
The dirtiness
& drudgeryness
O' th' world.

i.

Stork scissors are the progeny of 19th-century
umbilical clamps, used to stem the flow of blood
after birth. Forceps, twined with serpents, made
a handsome set for midwives, who would practice
needlework while waiting for the head to crown.
Busy fingers seed the evolution of instruments.

ii.

The stork is a symbol of good luck.
The stork flies at an altitude somewhere between here and heaven.
The stork departs Europe for Africa in summer and returns in the spring.
The stork has been known to hold a bundle in its mouth.
The stork will drop a newborn down a chimney.
The stork has delivered three children to Mirka
        and has returned for its tithe.

iii.

She receives revelations by hand, her paints
and pens disclosing a figment or a phantom
of her womb in the shape of a pear—*surprise!*

She thinks on the pincer clamped around
her organ while she slept on the operating
table—it must have been a hungry beak

that ferried the fleshy tissue across the divide.
She spots a familiar outline on the shoulder
of a young girl—*surprise!*

Down by the water were all the couples, because all the bars on the hill were closed. This side of the river looked towards the sun, so the end of the evenings was magic. Morning twilight is like a good kiss—there without exception, and then gone. While dusk lingers on what's come before, dawn threatens to take the past away.

They had met outside the sealers bar, and outside Michael stayed, with the Blacks, Irish and worst of the drunk children. Michael was drunk too and too drunk to remember Tangana's name. Tangana had known plenty of Michaels, more so in the past year. Michael's excitement was a sort of confidence. To him things felt preordained, like he was his own creator. If he thought something it was true, like the world was changing and he was in it. That was his truth, and the colony's.

Frills and pink satin roughed up on cobblestone under lamp light. Tangana recognised the Irish thieves, caught posing as up-late women. Tangana loved to watch the men's loud behaviour, where laws seemed remade in the damp stone night, but law was the wrong word. This hole in language laughed, calling him in, like an open mouth. The mouth was wide and black.

The further they walked down the hill, the more the rocks gleamed and stank of blubber. When Tangana caught Michael's loose feet on the grease it was the first meeting of their lips, chins, hands, and mouths. It wasn't Michael's first time, but it was his first with a Crow. And so further down they went, until the private of the cove. Tangana took off Michael's boots. Lodged in his flesh was a shard of glass. This glass would outlast the evening, smoothed down by unending tides. Plucked then abandoned by wandering hands, the glass's lustre was mistaken for quartz, a local mineral now famous at the cove. Lit by the right light, the brochure said, it left everything sparkling at dawn.

excerpt from *She is the Earth* | ALI COBBY ECKERMANN

in the opaqueness
I glimpse whitecaps

surging towards me
at shoulder height

frigid I stand
awaiting impact

the frothy streaks
bubble and foam

yet never reach
a consternation

what is a threshold
if not a memory
I exist here
ready to enter
the door is closed

as thought subdues
keys appear in my eyes
admission is an opera
the crescendo of breath
is flight and I am away

excerpt from *Shouldering Pine* | BROEDE CARMODY

I'm not sure how much
time we have left on this spinning
rock in the sky,

I think, as a great gum reaches
for Orion's belt.
Just because a place is

beautiful doesn't mean you won't slip
down an abandoned mine
shaft. We're all panning

for specks of something.
A friend's tarot cards describe
the road I must take.

I explain that a raw chestnut tastes
like carrot. We walk back
to the Airbnb under a warm lick

of rain. In a way, we are all
mountains: emptying ourselves into rivers
emptying into the ocean.

It's funny how sadness always manages to hammer out a new shape.

Whenever I sit down into soil
part of me doesn't want to sit back up.

Plough shallow & you get
a worthless crop.

Not a symmetry of trees
in clear, straight lines.

What's the point if a fox is going
to come home anyway?

A hairbrush snapping in two
across the back of my skull.

There is a word for across the other side
of the river. It isn't my place to tell you.

If you're lucky, a phone tower
won't block your view.

Is that moss, or a bruise?
It's hard to tell if the space between

us is getting larger
or if it's just the universe expanding.

There's a reason I won't let you touch my throat with both hands.

sidney nolan | SUSIE ANDERSON

here is not familiar Country
I love what I see but don't recognise
anyone who has spent time with this land knows
the gleaming is practical
fields either side of well-worn roads
driven after school or between runs
to ballet class or piano lessons
site of harvest
so memory empties when called forth
mostly silent or low to ground among
peaks of earlier times blurred now with loss
where has this peach, this red come from?
plains echo ancestral
he must have meant an everyday blend
gold and grey with blue haze horizon
gestural motion of strokes rings true at least
recalls heat of endless January
giving every direction its own pulse
I long to inhabit that edge

Sixth Sense | THABANI TSHUMA

The first movie with a major plot twist I witnessed was
The Sixth Sense—
Where we find out Bruce Willis's character was dead the whole time.

That specific twist is a trick I learnt to live my life by.
See, addiction is a haunting.
A relentless search for peace by someone who's long been deceased.
A stillborn self-image clawing for a breath of life.
It's making bedmates of death's darkness.
So, Step into my shadow.

Where a needle prick, pill drop or whiskey shot acted as a rusty crowbar
trying to pry open my soul
to feel something.
To feel anything at all.
Anything but dead.
Days turned to nights turned to weeks turned to years,
searching to feel alive!
So, of course, I took to poetry,
to hitting line
after after line
after line
after lying to myself
after battling denial
after trying to put back together the scattered jigsaw fractal pieces of my
mind.

I'm trying to be honest these days,
trying to tell my story like is,
unfiltered, triple distilled just how I like it.
I mean *liked*.
I'm ashamed of how much I liked it.
Of finding an ecstatic sweet relief,
and how that mattered more than living,
mattered more than loving, and all it leaves is longing:
one more hit,
one more sip,
just one kiss,
just tonight,
just forever.
They say we spirits, we live forever.
What that means is that the dying is never-ending
and that the living is spent pretending.
Covering up the pooling crimson quagmire of my fatal wound,
blending in as one of them who assumes,
HIM??
there's no way he could be consumed by phantom antics.
And if he is
call it possession,
a phase,
an escape
anything to lessen this waking funeral truth.

I buy into it too,
walking both sides of this realm.
An abject detective solving my own murder.
I am both Sisyphus and the boulder.
At the precipice of perception both
the eye and the beholder.
It's impossible to hold the incorporeal closer.
I spend my days hugging wraiths.
I faced my inner demons to be haunted by the ghosts of overdoses,
I still hear them screaming,
Thabani call me,
Thabani hold me,
Thabani save me.
I can not save you,
I'm dead too.

But I don't know it.

Getting clean has been a graveyard.
I'm groundskeeper frantically digging,
measuring 6 feet while shovelling twelve steps.
I keep digging,
and digging,
and digging.
My past won't stay buried, but My friends do.
We spectres don't remember who we were before we died.

I'm trying to recover that.

There is no call to action,
no solemn catharsis,
no sympathy for the strung out.
I'm just a kid with a blanket pulled to his chest, talking to ghosts.
And I wonder if anyone also look at folks like me
croaking the twisted ghastly gasp to ghouls that goes,

I see dead people.

Scan QR code to watch Thabani Tshuma
perform this poem on ABC Arts's *Slammed.*

'Omg B you're frothing on life in this pic. S get with the program!'
said M on the group chat, in regard to S and B
on a boat in Mykonos: the sea off-sky colour,
the sky off-sea, the horizon softly conflicted with
reverberations in the ridges of the breastbones of the pelicans
to which the flight muscles are attached. To which the birds are
  attached to flight.
S's smile is definitely the lesser. They both look well:
we've come a long way from the eerie niche of skin cells
more sensitive to light, and our sore eyes and our heart-eyes
pore over their sphere from an ultrasea unbroken distance.
There are no angels only spasms, protective, unbidden;
B's smile is beautiful, a bit berserk, but not for long.
Content inside sincerely modest pain, the middle course,
we've been made mild with semi-cures, because science
smiles on its bishes, on us and the patient zero of the Black Death
which science recently ran to earth near Lake Issyk-Kul
in Kyrgyzstan. In stone: 'It was the year of the tiger. Here is the tomb
of the believer Sanmaq. He died of pestilence.'
Did he ever. We've caught the double smiles. And think of pelicans:
ridiculous, yet at the end of their high dives
their necks don't snap because a great federate spasm of muscle
protects them. And they lead with their water knives.

Aomori Prefecture doesn't stage the
Self-doubt you assumed it would once
You've revived the piece
As 'The Sound of Hammering'.
You think Dazai would telegraph
From an Iwate seaside hot spring
A molten grimace, then catch sight
Of the wrath of Sappho
After the Peloponnese forest ignition.
Right. Doubt. A hollow sting singing in the
Original, on the path to a Tokyo borough.

These finches have a monopoly on the remaining worms
At the edge of the trail cut into the dwarf bamboo by the bears.
So, name the ringing bell and give it its sonorous due.
Call it '*Ding-Ding-Ding*' or '*Bang, Bang, Bang*'
Or even just '*Toka-Ton-Ton*', for crying out loud.
A flourishing of therapists from good suburbs
After the declaration. Glenda Jackson's unintentional
Heebie-jeebies. Banality of postwar evil.
The rattle in Mum's head when she starts that kind
Of sentence. I throw my teaspoon, audible
From across the sand plains, beyond the vineyards,
It's where you first come from, and thenceforth
Spalding Gray's Hudson. Wasn't it Hudson?
No, it wasn't. Jasmine hedges. There's no onomatopoeia
For the jangling of coins showering park-lining pavement,
Rolling along the embankment, marking the spot
Where they collide with the paper ship routes.

That's what Sydney Harbour Bridge meant to the lost magpies,
Even what an Australian morning might do to an Aomori departure.

No one told us that dodging the gold standard honours
Your ancestors. She calls us crazy
For sniffing out the bluff necropolis beyond the fields.
More of your countrypeople in the metropolis
Than in the salt of the earth you called homeland.
Even if they were skiffs of another breed, another
Manifestation of no one's siesta of the footy fathers.
Because a siesta means a footy siesta,
So you'd better throw a ball against the wall.
Comparatively, she doesn't really love me, of course.
I should have known in April, buying tickets.
Why does she insist. And why not. That's why we're
Building a theatre around this church of one.
Every great head is hollow, hence the hammering.
Toka-ton-ton after *toka-ton-ton* is harder to abide
In a university press. And yet I never once
Questioned that she did, love me as she does
With scowls of translation and her parents' love.

That's why this short story must be epistolary after
Imperial abrogation. A teacher's colloquial mistake.
That's why the lyric bends away from and within
The instrument in the cities. Like Magic Eye.
Remember those? Remember the kids who couldn't do it.

psych! fountain, six wavy lines
of plush rice and you're
fainting onto mounded cellulose
the wood pulp fermented
to voluptuous froth

you stand in a plastic tub
harvesting showers
                    laundry Aphrodite

levitate to save energy

                    pinpricks
     shadow stairs behind the bins
                    pinions

looking forward to an infinity
of small collapses
          gilded by their own intensity

contemporary intuition
I am enjoying being horizontal
          heard as *I'm reading Scott Morrison's horoscope*

pebble warm like organs
pill pack not a coin
dimples in the recollection
disrupted plots
breathless journalist
tours ASIO
the rumour file is a valid barometer

if we film ourselves
will we be noteworthy
or will future watchers
respond to the decor, the shirts
whether or not people smoked inside
parlance shifts and regularities
the thrall of a self-portrait
            is that you don't know what's coming

My great-grandfather liked to take things slowly
trailing the cows he bought in Terang back to Warrnambool—
a distance of 45 ks, all the while walking with his hands
clasped behind his back in the early part of the twentieth century
a man who fondled potatoes, rosary beads, was noted
in a newspaper obituary.
My brother and I learned to take it slow walking behind 120 Jerseys
along a back road of ferns and stringybarks, catching their big-boned swaying
rhythm
looking for a dawdling calm, following the leader
into bush country that had mostly been cleared.
In time, my brother and I came to know the curves and ridges of this road—
when to expect rabbits or an echidna bunched in the gravel.
We drove the cows 15 ks to Swan's Lane for summer feed, autumn
we walked them back, heavily pregnant, pausing uphill
from Brucknell Creek where the bitumen rises then drops, our futures
mapped by a herd that was ready to calve.
Each morning I like to take things slow—
release the pup from her crate, clean her mess
wipe down the black plastic floor mat.
Each action driven by cause and effect
following her out the sliding door, across the deck
down the concrete ramp to the back lawn.
She squats beside an apple tree, a routine that wakes me.
I pour pellets into her silver metal bowl, make coffee
stroke her back while she sniffs under the chair
I think of my great-grandfather
walking from Warrnambool to Ararat
to visit his daughter in the *lunatic* asylum. The kind of random thoughts
I followed sliding blocks of cheese along a conveyor belt—
tracing a pattern with my hands while thinking about something else.
Twice a year my great-grandfather tramped through bush

skirted the Hopkins, shifted through Hexham, Willaura
        to pay the fees for his *highly strung daughter*
one of many teenagers, housewives, women enduring mania
        of polite disposition, captured in grainy black and whites.
Insignificant, history-less women locked behind peep hole doors
        suddenly visible all these years later through stories I cannot trust.
Where was my great-grandfather taken on those walks to Ararat?
        Losing himself amongst the ferns, the way my brother and I mumbled
to each other, scuffing our rubber boots along gravel and bitumen
        my great-grandfather taking it slow along dirt tracks, his daughter, Minnie,
on laundry or kitchen duty for years, a woman who couldn't look after herself
        dependent on routine to wake her in the scrubbed linoleum wards.
I spoon some peanut butter into a Kong for the pup
        her restless energies, focused, calmed as the morning can ever be.

are opposed to the police. in ways
train squeezes steel tracks words grip
& trip over on the grimy bluestone
the gutted stars shift past our lantern
tongues / voices rattle against tin
chests & bless / yell swiftly over right
side back shoulder / how a horse
scared will mince quickly / back right
hearts wince & dream in frost-grey
lent / jasmine sheds. sydney cuts into
my asthma like a hammer. ovened-
up energies merge with over-cleaned
streets. versus bolshy lovers. bird-
bone prints in our pillows talk lightly
put stone-sweet sleep under grass

she existed in masks: lorikeets loudest in the mornings, leaves deliberating on a breezy day, blinds fluttering against the sill, the hum of conversation on the footpath by her window, Fleetwood Mac, her fingers on the keyboard (tippity-tap), her anxious dog's paws pattering on the floorboards, her husband's snoring at 3am, the off-and-on whir of the coffee machine, cafes cackling like campfire, firetruck sirens every 43-degree day. *maybe silence doesn't exist* she thinks. maybe silence is just a quietening, until feigned decibels reign: radio crackle between channels, a cicada stuck in cochlea's dusk. her castle in the cortex: an orchestra ringing Bach. no, a conductor signalling silence.

•

she existed in masks: lorikeets loudest in the mornings, leaves deliberating on a breezy day, blinds fluttering against the sill, the hum of conversation on the footpath by her window, Fleetwood Mac, her fingers on the keyboard (tippity-tap), her anxious dog's paws pattering on the floorboards, her husband's snoring at 3am, the off-and-on whir of the coffee machine, cafes cackling like campfire, firetruck sirens every 43-degree day. *maybe silence doesn't exist* she thinks. maybe silence is just a quietening, until feigned decibels reign: radio crackle between channels, a cicada stuck in cochlea's dusk. her castle in the cortex: a daily orchestra ringing Bach. no, a conductor signalling silence.

•

in the hum of her
keyboard sirens every day
she crack s the signal

To Learn a M/other Tongue | DŽENANA VUCIC

I learn sustenance first:
trešnja, jabuka, mlijeko, hljeb
learn to say nisam gladna before
I can say that I am, learn that I
must leave food uneaten since
empty plates are want to be
filled with samo malo još

Then comes movement
(dolazimo, idemo, hajmo mi,
moja ćerka je došla)
and the whiplash of names,
which sound familiar but are not,
and which suggest directionality
or, at the very least, direction

In the stillness that follows
I learn to call things—stol, drvo
list, cvijet, nebo. My father is a
translator, he touches objects
and turns them to sound, stretches
his arms across naše selo and
renders the world legible

Speaking the self comes slow,
and without intuition. I am not
cold, ali hladno je. To know the
difference I must know when
to uncouple myself and when to
double back. I do not miss you,
ali nedostajao si mi

Grammar comes slower yet and
forces us into the perpetual
present. There is always someone
missing and we can never be
sure who did what to whom since
I conjugate poorly and without
regard to grammatical gender

in any case, we do not burden
ourselves with syntax. There is too
much history to get lost in semantics
and we are more interested in
the little things: gdje si, šta radiš,
je si ti gladna? Hajde, hoćes ti kafu?
Drago mi je što si došla

Glossary/Pronunciation

Note: Bosnian is written such that every letter is said. It is difficult to render this for English speakers, particularly for words like 'drvo' and 'gdje'.

Trešnja (tresh-nya) – cherry
jabuka (yah-bu-kah) – apple
mlijeko (mli-jeh-koh) – milk
hljeb (hlyeb) – bread
nisam gladna (knee-sahm glahd-na) – I'm not hungry (feminine)
samo malo još (sah-moh ma-loh yosh) – just a little more
dolazimo (doh-lah-zi-moh) – we're coming
idemo (i-deh-moh) – we're going/leaving
hajmo mi (high-moh mi) – let's go
moja ćerka je došla (moya cher-kah ye dosh-lah) – my daughter has come
stol (stohl) – table
drvo (drvoh) – wood/tree
list (list) – leaf
cvijet (svi-yet) – flower
nebo (neh-boh) – sky
naše selo (na-sheh sell-oh) – our village
ali hladno je (ah-li hlad-noh ye) – but it's cold
ali nedostajao si mi (ah-li neh-doh-sta-yao si mi) – but I miss you (lit: you are missing to me)
gdje si (gdye si, often spoken as 'jessi') – where are you (common greeting in Bosnian)
šta radiš (stah rah-dish) – what are you doing?/what are you up to?
je si ti gladna? (yeh si ti glahd-nah) – are you hungry?
Hajde, hoćes ti kafu (high-deh hoh-chesh tik kah-fu) – come on, do you want coffee?
Drago mi je što si došla (drah-goh mi ye si dosh-lah) – I'm glad you came

Topography | *KRIS HEMENSLEY*

22/11/21 Northcote — All Nations Park back
of Coles shopping plaza —Degani's take-
away coffee or la famiglia dine-in bespoke
pizza cold-drinks cappuccino cream-pastries —
sit on bench beyond cafe where π.o. joked
"old Greeks" decamped —out of dark
interior looking back from sun bathed park
an ululating moozik —name it rebetika
as if old Greek except for momentary oblique
must be Italian —neither Turk nor Iraq/
Baghdadi descanting Ahmed Hashim's bark
at same moon & stars same night —
wine-all-gone ache as any might
wake with —too broke too tired too late
to buy more —would sooner croak
than beg —here in this world its flocks
of beggars -slipping stratae agreed- hacks
with pens & notebooks the poets of Bacchus'
house temple his devotees —mine too
(Mike Dugan in '68 urging on us Hal Porter's
Watcher on the Cast Iron Balcony
in midst of Liverpool Scene & Beats at least
to know past & present Melbourne he said —
read again now to know our late friend?

(jump genre & generation —jump pages
(disbelieved the 6th while signing Covid register
at Degani's retraced to the 3rd —but it's December
14th! (tell whom now? the adjacent
that is the necessary ear —who can i tell?
(thank you loves —comrades —the interminable
hollow hour (Heather: "this broken night" —
Chrissie: "our embattled family" —
shock horror
-im memoriam-
John Nolan died Dec 13th
Matty: "big brother to us Godboys, forever
grateful" [topography rewritten
9/12 —corrections
& additions —
(wiser after the event —
(always tell everything
Dec 15, '21
fin

i. calendar

the courtyard rat squatting
on an empire of pizza boxes
rainsoaked piles of stewing
cardboard   flattened packaging
from long covid's eager merchandise
anything to transcend an unimagined
plague   rat traps line the walls like
doctors' obsolete portmanteaux from
a much earlier decade   just what is
happening here the green parrot quizzes
perched high on an empty branch of a terminal
tree waiting for the developer's paunch to crush
its trunk   a cold slab of fermented porridge rises
over the neighbourhood like a putinesque moon

what rabid declensions
resurrect under this
demography of tongues
the chocolate of the world
disintegrates

ii. chew

after the rain a boring
feeling comes   dampness
flattens the view like a
page of mediocre poetry –
the harbour has lost its
aureole   grey grey i
hate you grey   danked
buildings shrunk against
a shoddy sky   down in the
drains rats chew through
the postcodes

Two Thousand and One Nights | PETER ROSE

Surely it must abate soon.
Catullus can't go on writing
those rubbishy poems forever.
How they creak like arthritis.
Surely they must dry up eventually.
Year after year he pops up in journals
that tolerate his fetishes, his creepy anniversaries.
Yet Lesbia has no memory of those rites,
denies ever having had a relationship with him.
I mean, did anyone in Rome ever see them together?
            So she thinks to herself
on the eve of her umpteenth wedding,
swishing along the terrace in a Gucci kaftan,
younger than springtime, as they say.
Will poor, stubborn Catullus never move on,
never heed what she told him ad infinitum?
Is there no one who can assuage him?
How long can a poet catastrophise
such love, if that's what it was?
            Not a bit of it, Lesbia.
If I must suffer those dreams,
wake endlessly moaning your name,
endure your emasculating taunts,
I'll write a hundred more poems—no, a thousand—
make that two thousand and one,
just for old time's sake—such was our ardour,
now become the rancour of nostalgia,
just a warped, public simulacrum
of our callow, irregular love.

Untitled Wild Geese Game | VIDYA RAJAN

[sorry Mary Oliver] [sorry House House]

you do not have to be good
(you are horrible)
you do not have to walk on your knees
(you have no knees) (your feet are webbed)
for a hundred miles, through the desert repenting
(only a few miles, it's a village after all, and
it's a lovely morning and
you are a horrible)

thinking about who gets to be bad

like geese… or some children
or some leaders
and their closest followers. very few
of the people I know enjoy
the grace of mistakes.
they'd probably love a gentle historical
wave of the hand,
less assumed responsibility, less criminal glance,
less epigenetic markers of this or that
shithole country of origin stress –

Honk! Honk!

thinking of knees, thinking of scraping them,
getting my fifth tetanus shot – *why'd the brits leave*
so much scrap metal – was it our own fault – we should
have cleaned it up – and
pinching the puffy permanent scar from my third-world vaccine

it's hard to make good decisions when you want to be bad

stealth mode, if only

relatedly, sometimes I'm tempted by dominion
over the prairies and the deep trees
the mountains and the rivers
but then, I remember:
the world doesn't offer itself to our imagination

Honk! Honk!

choose smaller.

« if we make a wrong decision, everything will turn to absolute dust »

so I'm letting the harsh animal of my body, like –
so I'm complaining all the time, cute –
so I'm pissing angrily in my own toilet, ew –
so I make this farmer cry, wah wah,
the chud,
and I steal all the bells, ALL of them,
for my very own special ditch,
the village has no clue but yes, the rumours are true, it is me:

~ the most horrible, the most best, the most wildest of goose ~
~ I'll never be lonely again ~

and then I'm walking the few metres up and down
our tiny carpeted apartment, and you're
off to another appointment, in the crumbling animal
of your own body, and you're saying something like
well, when we were young we didn't have
all this, and the rice, the grains, if you trace them back,
were of poor quality, the best exported elsewhere,
for the empire?
and now all these illnesses, I guess I guess

I can barely hear
I just want a new noise that's all, um:

Honk me to the moon!
Let me honk among the stars!
Let me see what honk is like on
Jupiter and Mars!
Weightless and unflappable – probably!
(in the history and family of things)

1.

Verrition: an untranslatable term Césaire used to indicate a kind of sweeping. Not really: it was a term to indicate the double *jouissance* of licking words, over and over again. But that is not unlike sweeping, and sweeping is not unlike action painting, your heft and back pushing bristles as they sound off, marking the floor with a tacky rub, or licking the ground, over and over again.

Maybe we could buy a new broom at Bunnings? That question hovers for minutes, days. Maybe we could find ourselves licking the ground at the interval between days, between minutes, between the 59 and the 0? What is the interval between days, between night and day? (*Le petit matin*, Césaire called it, which Walcott translated, and I find plausible, as *foreday morning.*) Cognitive drowning, or a tortured landscape in foreday morning, then. Drowning before or at the fore of the zero, which is day. What I mean is that this is not the only thing tethered to the fore of a zero thing, the foreday thing, which is not only an aesthetic thing. And the inclusion of human references here will not be decorative. Except the conclusion here might be decorative, assuming the human will have already existed.

I can't open it, I say, when I can't open a file or a link, when I don't have the password anymore. I can't open it anymore. But then I thought I was in a landscape or countryside. The file or the link was in the countryside. How do I open a link out there? What if I don't know the password? What if I don't know the countryside—which countryside—the institutional countryside—that has disordered my relationship with passwords? My body seizing, pushing bristles as they sound off. This would be me, from the countryside.

Glissant says, I am less interested in your origins in the countryside than in how you would draw a tree, for instance, which is no longer genealogical nor biographical when the picture includes the soil, the manure, the grasses, the birds, the water in the air, the water in the ground, the water on the leaves, the adjacent trees, all the condensation from all the leaves, the clouds humming in the blue hinterland. Humming is historical. Is it biographical, but no longer intimate? Or is it intimate, but no longer personal; that is, no longer a person? Waiting for a live one in a tortured landscape: humming. This is not Glissant talking anymore, this is someone else. This would be me. The notion of privacy is an intensely held public notion; quite the sacred notion, if a notion can be spoken about as sacred. This morning me and my notion tentatively called the Magistrate's Court, passing through a number of institutional countrysides into the sacred countryside where the private matter could be dealt with. Then, more boldly, we called the Carpet Court. We ordered 59 kilometres squared of carpet. We wanted to lay it down and lick the ground, over and over again.

2.

At some point I try to tally roughly how many times I texted 'Leo is leaving this Monday' or 'Leo left this Monday', usually prefaced with 'I'm not sure if I already told you, but—' or suffixed with '—I thought you should know'. Three times would have been ideal. I went for a walk at night in Lorne, at some point I thought to do it, as a context. Shape of the bay and shape of the moon, plausibly analogous. A plausible analogy. An old Italian man in my car is at me about poetics, because it takes me a long time to understand things I love. A woman eats a rotisserie chicken. One hand holds the chicken. The other hand, covered in a plastic bag, prises the flesh apart. Her mouth holds something key—the neck?—in place. I wear the new PSG jersey to the little bar they have here and the staff at the bar go absolutely nuts. They go absolutely nuts. Which was probably, somehow, key: the neck of the plan.

Last night on the phone to Cam he told me he was the Ian Thorpe of chillin' and I said, yep, you're the chill-pedo and we both laughed and laughed, because my god there were so many levels to it. Like, two levels! And then because I was already getting off the phone I said, how the fuck can you follow chill-pedo, and at the same moment Cam said, who the fuck can I call now?

3.

The thing with protest is that it involves a lot of singing. Protest is the thing that involves a lot of singing. I am sitting on the Rathdowne St side of Carlton Gardens, near the corner of Victoria Pde. I have just finished work and I'm wearing my stupid work clothes, which protect me from being mistaken for a member of Extinction Rebellion, who set up camp here only a few hours ago only a few metres away. The XR camp is enclosed by an improvised fence made of washing line from which XR logo-ed tee-shirts hang. When I sit down, a trio of women are singing the Stop Adani song and I'm reminded of the claim I overheard once at a meeting to organise a protest immediately following the detention of DW embassy leader, DT Zellanach. Some guy in a wide-brimmed hat and hiking clothes was rifling through his soft briefcase full of sheet music, explaining to a pondy young woman that he is responsible for a number of the 'current chants', and that his authorship extends to 'Coal, don't dig it / Leave it in the ground it's time to get with it'. I don't know why I don't believe this easily plausible claim. The same week I attended that meeting about DT Zellanach, a local squatter in the house near the bike track told me he is currently involved in several legal cases, including one with Jay-Z for part-songwriting credit for Rihanna's 'Umbrella'. He told me this after asking me if I worked for the local council, thinking he was about to tell me to get fucked, concerned about the meaning of my work clothes. That claim about 'Umbrella' is a claim I am willing to entertain because it's more entertaining and therefore more plausible.

A few police shift about in the park, looking embarrassed, perhaps by XR's singing or perhaps by their own patrolling. They are humming, their own singing. I keep going to these things, though I keep reverting to this abstract journalism. Patrolling the singing, oh, the bloody singing: this is a wild desire to leave. Though we believe it when the protestors say this is an emergency.

There is a 'smoking area' that XR has set up near a river red gum outside the tee-shirt fence. On the back of a placard, the painted words say: 'Smoking Area: Bin Your Butts!' I stare at this sign for a long time. Under the river red gum, a young man and a young woman are slowly, but slowly, kissing. Last time I looked at them, before I began staring at the Bin Your Butts sign, they were simply staring into each other's eyes, legs crossed. I can't decide whether it is weird or completely unweird that everyone at the XR camp is white. I can't decide if it's weird that I wear a suit to work when there's no dress code at work and basically no-one ever sees me at work and, basically, I'm not even sure I'm really in work.

As I leave for my conventionally parked and recently washed car, I see the XR march coming up Exhibition St, singing the Stop Adani song. People clap on beat. People beat a drum. A police car parallel parks in the space behind me. The song sounds like what I imagine a dirge must sound like. Only now I realise I've never knowingly heard a dirge before. The policeman in the car scrapes his left wheels against the kerb. He nearly doors a cyclist. I have a feeling I shouldn't leave. The feeling is a dirge.

As I drive away, the radio plays an article about how the number of volunteer firefighters has been in decline since Black Saturday, in part due to the trauma of that event, in part because the weather is changing in a way that's unpredictable, so that no training can prepare someone to do this job. The weather is changing. Verrition, over and over: something so plausible I'm swept away.

Conclusion

The water in the kettle is dancing, says Leo. Can I use that, I ask.

Do you guys have any money, I ask. Cash money. Good point, says Mel, walking a $5 note to the man sitting on the ground in our path. Actually, I say, I want to go use the photobooth on the other side of the station. It only takes one- and two-dollar coins. Six bucks for four photos, I say. This is taken as a passing comment, because we never cross the bridge to the photobooth, not heading out west and not coming back east to the car.

We should go to the Skydeck when this is over, I say. The path to the Skydeck crosses our path, reminding me of the time I went to the Skydeck in a fever after speaking at the photography college. I'm afraid of heights, but sure, says Mel. That feeling of heights, explains Leo, is the body recalling a previous experience of falling. You feel it in your groin, I say. Yes, they both say. The past is a feeling in the groin, no-one says.

Somewhere after Queensbridge we lose our bearings following the river west. In an alcove under the Bolte Bridge, a department relevant to the river or the bridge has left a notice on a door. Do not venture further, it says. We look at the West Gate Bridge, which is closer than we remember. It's a destination we don't make this day, but a few days later those boys will get there. It doesn't make it to the news, but when they make the middle of the bridge, those boys start dancing.

Wasp | AMY CRUTCHFIELD

I hung like a fig
wasps eat from the inside
fruit in the shape of a tear
a purple chamber filled with flowers

wasps eat from the inside
buried in the soft red flesh
a purple chamber filled with flowers
I cannot paint it

buried in the soft red flesh
naked, alive, and unashamed
I cannot paint it
what made me unmakes me now

naked, alive, and unashamed
on a tree with blood like burning milk
what made me unmakes me now
nemo dat quod non habet

on a tree with blood like burning milk
you cannot give what you do not have
nemo dat quod non habet
faith is not enough

you cannot give what you do not have
I hung like a fig
faith is not enough
fruit in the shape of a tear

The morning men fill the fine lines across new paved cement, cracked by small breaks, like arid earth, marked by grey epoxy. The window calls up this view, backward to the benchtop where I stand, head bowed in the sink, washing chicken skin and carrots, a break of birdsong lifts my eye towards the cavern. Before the adjoining room, there was glisten; tufts of grass pressed to the bordering fence. Small freesias dot the line. A weaverbird made home in a neighbour's palm, that hung the height of the rooftops.

Water boils a whistle, a blue mug in the drying rack airs with yesterday's geography, a steady hand to the lip, I reach for the sometimes, the always of this room. Its continuity. A place I did not care for, but cared to look through; I was standing in this other room, at a previous time, thinking about one day standing, as I am now, standing and looking out again to the small bird weaving a nest-home against the reassurance of morning dew; its disappearance, plaster walls concealing the familiar scene, running tandem with my return, burdens my past with a newness, unburdens me now.

I look down towards the patterned cement and its associations. River-lines, a knot untangling, twin roads towards the sea's eclipse. The white of the adjoining wall, the small window, outside's promise, further and distant, like, the promise of my hand on your shoulder. I remember how I messaged you about my childhood kitchen. I was in a store, thinking about buying you a book, looking down at its innocuous cover as the view out the entrance; the hint of foliage hanging over the hold; the wind, animating the leaves, made a silent sound in my direction—held me forward towards this enclosure, I now coalesce within. You were far then. Your city, 'hot, dry and when it rained, it rained with you.' With your humming sadness that I searched up to, crawled upon, and watched your demotic hands turn a page. My hands too. Your chest left small marks on my cheeks that you thought to photograph—there was no camera. Instead, you traced a word across my face with a finger, slipping into my mouth, slipping further down, slipping between us, between verbs, amidst conversation overheard from the hallway, like a collection of small tiles, the room, porous grout.

Guy, we'd pass in the kitchen, my legs exposed and barefoot at the kettle, his greyed counterface and weighted hands on the stem, straining water and granule; he'd quip, each morning was nothing but another in a trail of others, hardened chips of paint, white and flaky, dalmatian the back of his hand. His mother had just died. He drank his coffee, leaving, always, his mug in the basin; I'd carry back into our room, cups of tea, and a foreign weight that you asked me to put down. To you, I'd said, isn't his Time, just as much, mine? Maybe you couldn't see what I did, through a crack in his door, his skin rough against the bed, clothes strewn the floor, and a face, indented with lines, a photograph of his old girl, pinned to the wall, six in a row, six under. Then, I still saw my mother as unable to cry. At her mother's bedside, composed and close to break, I thought a way to tell you about Guy, why I cared so much for his proximal, distant life. I saw water, contained and warm, pass from my hand to his. I saw him demure to the very present of his mother dying, and, I see myself, a spectator to her nurse, lay made up hands on her body, with more knowing than I could. Her head was cold. I whispered, B just had a baby, and mopped her brow, surprised by my feeling of wanting new life. Her chest, filling with fluid, breath laboured, her last light in the moon's full din. Day-old chapati, bruised nectarines, tableau of grapes, errant still life, a corner table that I kept to, to remember. There were sounds too, of childhood evening prayer, pausing play to prostrate on wet grass, released her body like a swollen breast to feed us. Come home. She is dying, said her voice, through the phone; she sounded how she used to, calling us in from the street, our outlines drawing clear, walking towards her in the pitch black.

I buried my head in my hands, listening to your mumble, your look for something to eat. Shirtless, shoulders drawn inside the open fridge, pulling potatoes out one by one, tumbling to the sink, washing their detritus down the drain, peeling their leather skin, lips in a slight pout at the tide drawing back, not knowing when it would return to shore. You were all of my summers, before I met you. There was nothing left to talk about knowing there was no more time. You turned towards my slumber with, 'Guy is gutless for arranging those photos of that woman,' and I agreed, for want of agreement. It was morning, anyhow; we both longed for the comfort of the morning after, and in your face, carrying small wets to the chopping board, was a half-way pause, widening past my head. I sat straighter, and peered behind my shoulder to the aura aside me; there was our door-window, its usual view of trees, and grass, and lines, so I turned. Back to your still posture nodding slightly, a smile cresting across your face. You leaned into the sun's pith crossing your eye, turning your gaze curious, and in it, I saw you, hand me over to something else.

Wednesday at Gunyah | SARAH PEARCE

i'd like to count two million freckles
as a mindfulness exercise

fat yellow moon slung low across the water
jordan peterson says not beautiful

rosewater spreads across the sunset sky
brit mum still hopeful after four miscarriages, one in toilet

morning sun glints fierce and wide from the ripples
amber heard colluded with the dog

i wrap myself around my coffee as hard as i can
try to keep from lying
through my teeth

there's a tern sunning itself on the end of the jetty
victoria beckham says thin is old-fashioned

megan fox celebrates birthday wearing dress
if you mess with the beaver you get the cleaver

freezing sea winds upon impact
for a second i wonder will i make it

What me worry | LAURIE DUGGAN

1

he travelled through life like a stuffed toy on the bumper bar of a tow truck

2

they glare through the recto of every bloody page

3

the way a line suggests
a scooting dog, the way
a cat arches, facing
a whistling kettle

blocked out shapes
of Böcklin's 'Island of the Dead'

4

let's go
move around these apostrophes
a semblance of order
the night watch or a shelf of onions
a possible apparel
caught on a small table in a large room

5

hands move over the baby's face
the baby doesn't notice

the poets publish
their collected works

a wall against
what future?

6

the authors of *Days of 49*
no longer with us

remember Gavin walking the two creeks with Frances
Alan with Geraldine in Gloucestershire
on the outside table an ashtray
piled the next morning with butts,

who else? Roy,
before the hill where three shires meet:
cut away beyond the horizon, a quarry

Lee who appeared in a moth-eaten tiger suit,
the days of 06

Wheatmania | FIONA HILE

Meet my corrals of farming future,
my pets, my friends and, at times,
my masters. Buzzing at the silly ghoul.
Single self-seeding sweet pea
forestalling global disgrace.
The wasteland. I don't miss it.
Hydrocolloid pimple patches
pressing howl and release
sheep drowning in a timbered lake.
I don't know what you get out of hurting me.
Undertaking numerous ring readings,
analysing your lunulae for signs of affection.
Requiem for a forgotten syllable
staged in memory of a township matinee.
Your vorticist train filter unsolves
Stations of the Cross. Not only what is kept
secret phylogenetic fantasy of tyranny,
the silent companion.

I'll bring them up — I am cheered by the boars of Rome. From here they look like citizenry (it's their familial filing) travelling purposefully on Via Tronfale, exerters of rights (quite different from right). It's not exactly that they lack rectitude; they have no morality, and no bind. Right now, we're glad for that, for their sake. An article describes them as strutting but I think their gait is pretty modest, and quite level, though a trot enough to cause vocal tremors. It's really their merging, grating voices that make me laugh, and please me, constant as the boars go. Roughly: not only 'come on, Tino' and 'Emilia, I'm here', but also: 'yes' 'I'm here' 'it's me' 'I am' 'I am'.

(Anyway) whose toes are they stepping on? In the video, none but their own. Although a woman does report that *i cinghiali* take up one side of the street and jump on her. Is she vertical or horizontal when this happens? In Barcelona, two boars steal Shakira's bag and take it to the woods. (No I am I am sympathetic but outrage is pedestrian).

Windscreen | JO LANGDON

Rear-windscreen soars ahead in status
vehicle tint, against which letters
in masking tape tatter: *TOOT*

TO GIVE DAN THE BOOT —only
some tape has come away
or a wiper obscures so that *B* becomes *R*.

There are those who would if they could
either way, I guess, but perhaps don't
know now

whether to toot. No horns sound
across the lanes, in either case. Behind me
the baby peels mandarins

she won't eat, admires her own toes
in reflection. These are

'donut days': no new cases
in the garden state, and time
before the premier's fall

from holiday
patio—time unfolding, eliding—
It's true in this state

we like our racism
covert, thanks, we like it
polite—

Beyond the radio's fizz
of numbers & brighter
airings, the state commits

cultural genocide—another
highway cutting three minutes
out of 800 years

or its inverse: that is to say
decimating what the colony has

plundered, heedless/knowing/
ceaseless/ly.

The light is yellow is green is falling
orange across us, encapsulated
between twisting figures

of tea-tree & box gum, detritus
of citrus skin & pith amassing.
Arundhati R wrote the pandemic

as a portal but I don't know how
to hold the image—where
to meet it.

winter jumper | HASIB HOURANI

for daniel, who was kind

shaking in a cotton shirt waiting for the tram to take me to work
i want a wool jumper so i can stop hating winter

we're walking home on eid al fitr and the lights are out
i am trying to brainstorm a way to afford a 100% wool jumper

i want mittens like the children wear:
windbreaker skin and fleece organs
gutsy fuschia inside and out

i am using my spare ten minutes to get lunch
i am stopped with a tote bag of things i didn't pay for
i am in trouble

if you get caught stealing your ten dollar lunch from woolies QV:
they cannot   make you pay for everything twice
they cannot even make you pay for everything once
        you can even leave everything at the kiosk and walk away

we're walking home on eid al fitr and i joke
that i could write a poem to subsidise the 100% wool jumper

the man who makes the sushi says i should be ashamed
the security guard smirks and frowns like a villain
                    she is 3 centimetres from my face
the woolies clerk tells me not to worry and reshelves my yoghurt

i want to stop hating winter but i don't have the 100% wool jumper

i'm shaken from being caught
handing out the cookies i paid for
because i did not leave everything at the kiosk and walk away

and now i'm in an e-meeting
with a lady who works for council
telling her *pay your artists* and naming
(3) places that assign liveable rates
which my workplace does not offer
(it's not their fault i promise)

i want to stop hating winter but last year
my power bill did that thing that cells
do when they double in thin air

thank you gds for paying me $100
now i can buy the 100% wool jumper
now i can stop hating winter
thank you daniel for shelving my yoplait so simply

i go to work / i go to work / i go to work / i go to work / i go to work / dilan says – i love you dad / dilan says – but i love mum more / i go to work / four days in a row / 5,6,7,8 / im tired / when i go home i also go to work but i dont say that / centrelink says sophie doesnt work / its a lot of work being a parent, people say / it must be a lot of work / how do you do it? they say, i cant imagine / but i go to work and i work / i come home and i work and i work / on fridays i dont go to work but when my dad asks i say – im at work – because i am, im writing, im working / sometimes i ride to work / sometimes i ride to work with dilan on the back and drop her at childcare / sometimes i run beside her as she rides / i walk to work / i drive to work / i catch the tram to work / i get dropped off at work / im yet to work from home, my industry doesnt allow it / sometimes i say to people that i go to work to rest, work begins when i get home / i say things like – i better go to work – im running late for work – i cant be bothered going to work today – sorry, ive gotta go to work – i just knocked off work / my payslip says i worked 30 hours this week / some people work 60 hours a week but im not impressed / sophie works 168 hours a week / my grandma, who they say never worked, said to me – work, ender, work a lot, work hard, you must work / my grandma worked, at home, from home / i call my grandpa from work on a sunday, i tell him im on lunch break, he is impressed – oooow, he says, very good / my grandpa worked until he did his back / my mum went back to work when i was 1 / my mum still works / the working class works / i go to work / the dishwasher works / this pen works / the cars getting fixed / this deodorant really works / does the ant work? / does the mushroom get time in lieu? / does this swimming pool ever relax? / this worker, it is said, works for the boss / works for the man / the nuclear family doesnt work / the father works / the mother labours / the child plays / the child gets schooled / the child is prepared for work / a guy i worked with said he needed 2 million bucks to retire / a work death balance / some people say they love their work / some people hate their life / i go to work / this must be a great place to work they say to me at work / we came to australia as workers / to work / australia is good for work, turkey is good to live, people say / australia might be a workers paradise / maybe this is a wonderland where each human received the basics of life, food shelter healthcare culture community / when i lived in turkey my music teacher said that hed only once been to another country, bulgaria when it was communist – how was it? i asked – fantastic, he said, people were out on the streets and in the bars drinking talking and singing every night

Today is the ninth day
of winter, my least favourite season
even though the light is special and hot
showers are pretty great. Lentil stew
with tahini and feta and toasted
seeds is also excellent. I wore two
pairs of socks and my feet felt trapped.
Even though I know it's gauche to complain
about the weather, I do it anyway. But this
poem doesn't care about the weather; this poem
cares about blackberries, which are sour and
delicious, and garden spiders who weave delicate
webs, and broccoli pasta with pickled chillies
and parsley, and the song 'Brimful of Asha
(Fatboy Slim Remix)' playing on the stereo,
which is to say it cares about what is good
as narrated by Arvind Rosa.

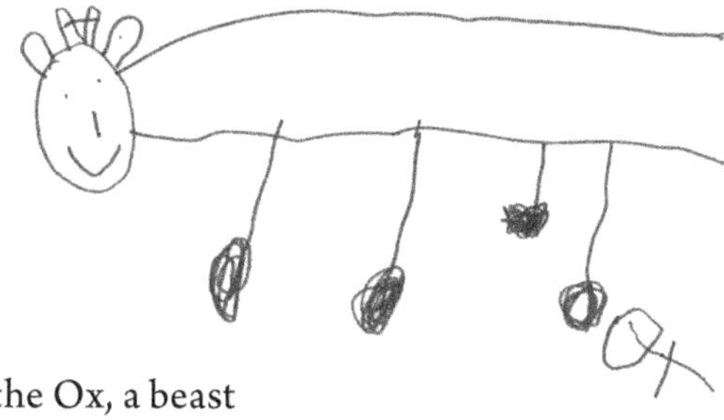

I was born in the year of the Ox, a beast
with a broad back and generous spirit who carried
the rat (and everything that critter carried, like gossip
and dreams and perversions, like handfuls of toasted almonds)
across the line. Before I was born, the last time
it was the year of the Ox was 1973, which gave us
'Crocodile Rock' and the first global
oil crisis, which also marks the beginning of the end
of US hegemony, even as some got high
huffing the fumes of circulation as if they were huffing
tulips in bloom. 'Crocodile Rock' is terrible song
that is perfect as a harbinger of doom. Later that year
Sly and Family Stone would release 'If You Want Me
To Stay', a song that feels so good you wish
you could live inside it, and you can, if only for
a moment. The alchemy of the three minute
song is that it is a container for all that is
uncontainable, like 'clouds, big ones oh it's
blowing up wild outside.' Two tides: 'Crocodile Rock'
and 'If You Want Me To Stay'. Is this what they
mean by the dialectic?

Note: For stanza one, I asked Arvind to draw and tell me things she loves, some of which made their way into the poem (spiders, broccoli pasta, 'Brimful of Asha (Fatboy Slim remix)', blackberries). Stanza two is much more straightforward—an image of an ox and a rat.
—ANDREW BROOKS

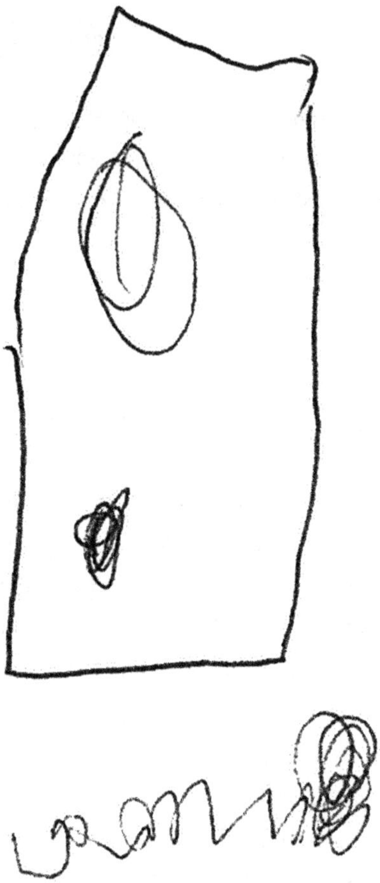

CONTRIBUTORS
& ACKNOWLEDGEMENTS

Notes on Contributors

Jordie Albiston was born in 1961, and grew up in Melbourne. She studied Literature and Women's Studies at La Trobe University, for which she received a PhD. She published fourteen poetry collections, three children's books and a handbook on poetic form. Two of her collections were adapted for musical theatre, both enjoying seasons at the Sydney Opera House. Albiston's work has been recognised by many awards, including the Mary Gilmore Award, the Wesley Michel Wright Prize and the NSW Premier's Prize. Albiston was honoured in 2019 with the Patrick White Literary Award and in 2022 (posthumously) received the John Bray Poetry Award in the Adelaide Festival Awards for Literature.

Susie Anderson is a writer of poetry and nonfiction whose work reflects on the hidden layers of visual arts practice, Country, memory and place. A proud Wergaia & Wemba Wemba woman from Western Victoria, her poetry and nonfiction writing has been published in a variety of publications in Australia and abroad, in print and online.

Louis Armand is a Sydney-born writer. His most recent collections of poetry include *DI/ODE I–CCCX* (2023), *VITUS* (2022), *Descartes' Dog* (2021) and *Monument* (with John Kinsella, 2020). His novels include *The Combinations* (2016) and *Abacus* (2015). His most recent volume of criticism is *Entropology* (2023).

Alison J Barton is a Wiradjuri poet widely published in Australian and international literary and poetry journals. Her poetry has been recognised in several prizes and appeared in *Best of Australian Poems 2022*. In 2023, she won three places at Varuna House and was the inaugural recipient of the Cambridge University First Nations Writer-in-Residence Fellowship, where she will write her second collection. Alison's first full-length collection of poetry, *Not Telling*, will be published in 2024 with Puncher & Wattmann.

Ender Başkan is a poet and bookseller. His book of prose *A Portrait of Alice as a Young Man* was published and distributed with the help of friends in 2019. His poems, essays and fragments have been published in *HEAT*, *Overland*, *Meanjin*, *Cordite*, *Unusual Work* and many other literary organs. In 2021 he won the *Overland* Judith Wright Poetry Prize. Sick Leave, Thin Red Lines and Liquid Architecture have hosted some of Ender's recent poetry performances.

Luke Beesley is a writer, artist and singer-songwriter. In addition to his highly regarded books, which include *Aqua Spinach* (2018), *Jam Sticky Vision* (2015) and *New Works on Paper* (2013), his poetry has been published widely in Australia and internationally and has been translated into several languages. His latest collection, *In the Photograph*, was published in 2023. He lives and works on Wurundjeri Woi Wurrung land (Naarm/Melbourne).

Judith Beveridge is one of Australia's most acclaimed poets. Winner of the Prime Minister's Literary Award and the New South Wales and Victorian Premiers' Awards, she is a highly regarded critic, editor and teacher of poetry. She has published seven collections of poetry, most recently *Sun Music: New and Selected Poems.* She is a recipient of the Philip Hodgins Memorial Medal and the Christopher Brennan Award for lifetime achievement in poetry. She was poetry editor for *Meanjin* from 2005 to 2015, and co-editor of the anthology *Contemporary Australian Poetry.*

Javant Biarujia is author of many books and chapbooks of poetry, including *Calques* and *Spelter to Pewter*, and is represented in more than twenty anthologies. He was Asialink's writer-in-residence in Indonesia in 1998, just after the fall of Soeharto. He is also an essayist, and prize-winning playwright. *Nainougacyou*, the dictionary of his constructed language, Taneraic, is his latest book.

Eva Birch has published her poems in *Cordite Poetry Review*, *Rabbit* and *Australian Poetry Journal*, among others. She is the founder of The Melbourne School of Literature, which she programs and teaches for. Eva is the author of *Megalodon* (Stale Objects dePress, 2019) and *Pearl* (Rabbit, forthcoming) and is currently working on a poetry EP.

Ken Bolton, a long-time employee of Adelaide's Experimental Art Foundation, has recently published *A Pirate Life* (Cordite Books) and *Fantastic Day* (Puncher & Wattmann).

Andrew Brooks lives on unceded Wangal land and lectures in Media and Culture at UNSW. He is a founding member of the Infrastructural Inequalities research network, one half of the critical art collective Snack Syndicate and a co-editor of the publishing collective Rosa Press. He is the author of *Homework* (2021), a book of essays on art and politics co-written with Astrid Lorange, and the poetry collection *Inferno* (2021). His current favourite snack is a handful of almonds, each with a drop of siracha sauce on top.

Arvind Rosa Brooks is five years old. She is into goal-keeping, music, guitars, reading, drawing, and riding her two-wheeled bike. She lives with her parents and cat on unceded Wangal country and if you come over to her house she'd like to show you her toys. She loves a little bit of chilli, and her current favourite snack is an anchovy straight from the jar.

Pam Brown has been active in the Australian poetry scene for decades. Her recent publications are *Stasis Shuffle* (Hunter Publishers, 2021) and *A Love Supreme*—a 2022 chapbook from Tim Wright's now orries press. Pam lives in south Sydney on Gadigal land.

Melinda Bufton is the author of *Girlery* and *Superette*. Her poetry has appeared in numerous publications, including anthologies *Contemporary Australian Poetry* (Puncher & Wattmann, 2016) and *Contemporary Australian Feminist Poetry* (Hunter Publishers, 2016). In 2019, she was the winner of the Charles Rischbieth Jury Poetry Prize as well as the Helen Anne Bell Poetry Bequest Award, the latter resulting in the publication of her third collection, *Moxie* (2020).

joanne burns is the author of numerous collections of poetry, including prose poems. Her most recent book is *apparently* (Giramondo, 2019). She is slowly assembling a new collection of her work, *rummage*. She lives in Sydney.

Broede Carmody is a poet from Dhudhuroa country in north-east Victoria. His first book, a collection of poems called *Flat Exit*, was published by Cordite Books in 2017. His poetry has also appeared in journals such as *Meanjin*, *Cordite* and *Voiceworks*. Previously, he took part in the Poet Laureates of Melbourne series (2020), was a co-judge of the Victorian Premier's Prize for Poetry (2019), was named among the Melbourne Writers Festival's 30 Under 30 (2017) and was a poetry editor for *Voiceworks* magazine (2012–2016). He is currently based in Melbourne.

Eileen Chong was born in Singapore of Hakka, Hokkien and Peranakan descent. She is the author of nine books. *We Speak of Flowers* is forthcoming with UQP in 2025. She lives and works on unceded Gadigal land.

Justin Clemens is the author of many books about philosophy, art, and poetry, including *Villain*, *Black River* and *The Mundiad*, which was shortlisted for the Kenneth Slessor Poetry Prize. His most recent poetry collection is *A Foul Wind* (Hunter Publishers, 2023). With Thomas H. Ford, he is also the author of the monograph *Barron Field in New South Wales* (University of Melbourne Press, 2023). He teaches at the University of Melbourne.

Ali Cobby Eckermann is a Yankunytjatjara poet and artist from South Australia whose work has been published and celebrated around the world. Her poetry collections include *little bit long time* and the award-winning collection *Inside My Mother*. Her verse novels are *His Father's Eyes* and *Ruby Moonlight*, which won the inaugural black&write! Indigenous fellowship, the Kenneth Slessor Prize, a Deadly Award and was named the NSW Premier's Literary Awards' Book of the Year. In 2013 Ali toured Ireland as Australia's Poetry Ambassador, and in 2017 she received the Windham-Campbell Prize from Yale University. She describes herself as a dreamer, a gardener, with deep respect for her journey thus far.

Alex Creece is a writer, collage artist, and average kook living on Wadawurrung land. Alex works as the Online Editor for *Archer Magazine* and the Production Editor for *Cordite Poetry Review*. She's also on the editorial committee for *Sunder Journal*. Alex has been awarded fellowships with Writers Victoria, Arts Access Australia, The Wheeler Centre and Midsumma Pathways. Her work has been shortlisted for the Kat Muscat Fellowship, the Next Chapter Scheme, the Geelong Writers Prize, the Born Writers Award and the Lord Mayor's Creative Writing Award. Alex's debut collection of poems is forthcoming with Cordite Books in 2024.

Amy Crutchfield's poems have been published in journals including *Island*, *Overland*, *The Moth*, *The Poetry Review*, *Westerly* and *APJ*. She won the Gwen Harwood Poetry Prize 2020/21. Her first collection, *The Cyprian*, was published by Giramondo in 2023.

Madeleine Dale is a Brisbane-based poet and researcher. She holds a first-class honours degree and Masters degree from the University of Queensland, where she is currently undertaking a PhD. Her first chapbook, *On Fire with Dangerous Cargo,* was published by Queensland Poetry in 2023. Her manuscript, *The Water-Bearers,* won the 2023 Thomas Shapcott Prize.

Shastra Deo was born in Fiji, raised in Melbourne, and lives in Brisbane. Her first book, *The Agonist* (UQP, 2017), won the 2016 Arts Queensland Thomas Shapcott Poetry Prize and the 2018 Australian Literature Society Gold Medal. Her second book, *The Exclusion Zone,* was published by University of Queensland Press in 2023.

Elese Dowden is a Pākehā writer and recovering philosopher living on unceded Wurundjeri land. Her poetry and criticism has been published in *Cordite, Meanjin, Overland, Rabbit* and *Landfall.* Elese's cross-disciplinary research interests include Australasian colonial history, comparative literature, critical theory and French philosophy. She also works as an organiser for the Melbourne School of Literature.

Dave Drayton was an amateur banjo player, founding member of the Atterton Academy, and the author of *British P(oe)Ms* (Beir Bua), *E, UIO, A: a feghoot* (Container), *A pet per ably-faced kid* (Stale Objects dePress), *P(oe)Ms* (Rabbit), *Haiturograms* (Stale Objects dePress) and *Poetic Pentagons* (Spacecraft Press).

Laurie Duggan was involved in the poetry worlds of Melbourne and Sydney through the 1970s and 80s. He lived in England from 2006 until 2018 when he returned to Sydney. His most recent books are *A Kite Hangs Above the Border* (Flying Islands, 2022), *Homer Street* (Giramondo, 2020) and *Selected Poems 1971–2017* (Shearsman, 2018).

Theodore Ell studied literature and modern languages in Sydney and in Italy. For several years he worked as an editor and translator and co-founded the international journal *Contrappasso.* From 2018 to 2021 Ell lived in Lebanon, accompanying his wife on a diplomatic posting. Ell's essay 'Façades of Lebanon,' about the Beirut port explosion, won the 2021 Calibre Essay Prize. His poetry collection *Beginning in Sight* shared the 2022 Anne Elder Award. He is an honorary lecturer in literature at the ANU.

Michael Farrell is from Bombala, NSW, and is based in Melbourne. Recent book publications include *Googlecholia* (2022) and *Family Trees* (2020), both from Giramondo. Michael has written chapters for the forthcoming *Cambridge Companion to Australian Poetry,* as well as for the *Cambridge History of Australian Poetry.* Michael's collages and other artwork can be seen on Instagram @ limechax.

Liam Ferney's collections include *Boom, Hot Take* and *Content.* His next collection, *The Darkest Timeline,* is forthcoming with Hunter Publishers. He lives with his wife and daughter in Brisbane.

Toby Fitch is poetry editor of *Overland* and a lecturer in creative writing at the University of Sydney. He is the author of eight books of poetry, including *Where Only the Sky had Hung Before* (Vagabond Press, 2019), *Sydney Spleen* (Giramondo, 2021), and, most recently, a newly expanded and full-colour edition of *Object Permanence: Calligrammes* (Puncher & Wattmann / Thorny Devil Press, December 2022). He co-edited *Best of Australian Poems 2021* with Ellen van Neerven, and edited the anthology *Groundswell: The Overland Judith Wright Poetry Prize for New & Emerging Poets 2007–2020.* He lives in Newtown on unceded Gadigal land.

Joan Fleming is the author of three books: *The Same as Yes* and *Failed Love Poems* (from Te Herenga Waka University Press), and *Song of Less* (Cordite Books). Her honours include the Biggs Poetry Prize, the Verge Prize for Poetry, the Harri Jones Memorial Prize from the Hunter Writers' Centre, a Creative New Zealand writing fellowship, and a residency with the Michael King Writers' Centre. Her manuscript *Dirt* was shortlisted for the Helen Anne Bell Poetry Bequest. She works as a lecturer in Creative Writing at Massey University, and writes about staying awake on the precipice of total ecological shitfuckery.

Zenobia Frost is a Brisbane poet. Her latest collection, *After the Demolition* (Cordite Books), unpacks the sharehouses of Brisbane. She won the 2020 Wesley Michel Wright Award and Queensland Premier's Young Publishers and Writers Award, and was shortlisted in the 2023 Gwen Harwood Poetry Prize. Along with fellow poet Rebecca Jessen, she edited the recent 'POP!' edition of *Cordite Poetry Review.*

Lou Garcia-Dolnik is a poet living and working on sovereign Gadigal Country. Their writing has been awarded Second Prize in the *Overland* Judith Wright Poetry Prize, a place on the shortlist for the 2020 Blake Prize, 2021 Val Vallis Award, 2022 LIMINAL Non-Fiction Prize, 2022 Kat Muscat Fellowship, and an Academy of American Poets University Prize from the University of Texas at Austin. They are the 2023 recipient of the Australian Poetry/NAHR Eco-Poetry Fellowship and recently attended Tin House's Summer Workshop.

Angela Gardner's verse novel *The Sorry Tale of the Mignonette* (Shearsman) was shortlisted for Wales Book of the Year, 2022 and a UK National Poetry Day recommendation. She has five other full-length poetry collections including *Some Sketchy Notes on Matter* (Recent Work Press, 2020), shortlisted for the Dorothy Hewett Award, and the Thomas Shapcott Prize winning *Parts of Speech* (UQP, 2007).

Kathryn Gledhill-Tucker is a Nyungar technologist, writer, digital rights activist currently living on Whadjuk Noongar boodjar. Their work explores the intersection of activism, science-fiction and technology in imagining radical futures and ushering them into existence.

Madison Godfrey is a writer, editor, educator, and the author of *Dress Rehearsals* (Allen & Unwin: JOAN, 2023). Their writing is described as 'sensual and often funny' by *The Guardian* and 'fiercely punk and undeniably powerful' by ArtsHub. Madison has performed poetry at the Sydney Opera House, the Royal Albert Hall, St Paul's Cathedral and Glastonbury Festival. They are a previous recipient of the Kat Muscat Fellowship, the Varuna Flagship Poetry Fellowship, and a Western Australian Youth Award for Creative Contributions to the state. Madison lives on Whadjuk Noongar land with a rescue cat named Sylvia.

Jake Goetz's most recent collection is *Unplanned Encounters: Poems 2015–2020* (Apothecary Archive, 2023). His first collection, *meditations with passing water* (Rabbit, 2018), was shortlisted for the QLD Premier's Award in 2019. He is the Reviews Editor at *Plumwood Mountain* and is currently undertaking a DCA at the Writing & Society Research Centre (Western Sydney University).

Lisa Gorton is a poet, novelist and essayist, and also works as an editor. She holds a doctorate on the poetry of John Donne from the University of Oxford. Her awards include the Wesley Michel Wright Prize, the Victorian Premier's Award for Poetry, the Philip Hodgins Memorial Medal, the Prime Minister's Award for Fiction (shared), and the NSW Premier's People's Choice Award for Fiction. Her most recent work is *Mirabilia* (Giramondo, 2023).

Rory Green is a writer, editor and digital media artist who grew up on Darkinjung land. Their email project *Otherwise Pokedex* aims to publish a poem for every Pokémon.

Natalie Harkin is a Narungga poet and Research Fellow at Flinders University living on Kaurna Yarta, South Australia. She engages archival-poetic methods to document community Memory Stories and decolonise state archives, and is a member of SA's inaugural State Records/State Library Aboriginal Reference Group. Her research centres on Aboriginal women's domestic service and labour histories, and Indigenous Living-Legacy / Memory Story archiving innovations for our time. Her words have been installed and projected in mixed-media exhibitions, including creative-arts research collaboration with *Unbound Collective*. Her manuscripts include *Dirty Words* (Cordite Books, 2015), *Archival-poetics* (Vagabond, 2019), and *APRON-SORROW / SOVEREIGN-TEA* (Wakefield, in-press).

John Hawke's most recent volume of poetry is *Whirlwind Duststorm* (Grand Parade, 2021).

Kris Hemensley is a writer & bookseller (Collected Works Bookshop 1984–2018; BookTreeHouse, 2019–Present). Has published many collections & chapbooks since 1967, most recently *Your Scratch Entourage* (Cordite Books, 2016) and *From The Blue Notebook* (now orries, 2022). *Topographies* is his work-in-progress since 2016.

Fiona Hile lives and works in Naarm Melbourne. Her first full-length collection, *Novelties,* was awarded the 2014 NSW Premier's Literary Awards Kenneth Slessor Prize for Poetry. Her second collection, *Subtraction,* was awarded the 2017 University of Sydney Helen Anne Bell Poetry Bequest.

Dan Hogan (they/them) is a writer from San Remo, NSW (Awabakal and Worimi Country). They currently live and work on Dharug and Gadigal Country (Sydney). Dan's debut book of poetry, *Secret Third Thing,* was released by Cordite Books in 2023. Dan's work has been recognised by the Val Vallis Award, *Overland* Judith Wright Poetry Prize, and XYZ Prize, among others. In their spare time, Dan runs small DIY publisher Subbed In. More of their work can be found at: 2dan2hogan.com.

LK Holt has published five full-length collections of poetry. Her book *Birth Plan* was shortlisted for the 2020 Prime Minister's Award for Poetry and the 2020 Victorian Premier's Award for Poetry. She is the recipient of the NSW Premier's Award for Poetry and the Grace Leven Prize, and has been longlisted for the Australian Literature Society's Gold Medal. She lives in Narrm/Melbourne.

Duncan Hose is a poet, painter and essayist. His published books include *Testacles Gone Walkabout* (Slow Loris, 2021), *The Jewelled Shillelagh* (Puncher & Wattmann, 2019), *Bunratty* (Puncher & Wattmann, 2015), *A Book of Sea-Shanty* (Bulky News Press, 2014), *One Under Bacchus* (Inken Publisch, 2011) and *Rathaus* (Inken Publisch, 2007). His first critical monograph, entitled *The Pursuit of Myth in the Poetry of Frank O'Hara, Ted Berrigan and John Forbes: Prick'd by Charm,* was published by Palgrave Macmillan in 2022.

Hasib Hourani is a writer, editor and educator. His debut book of poetry will be published by Giramondo in 2024.

Holly Isemonger is a poet from Gerringong, NSW. She was the joint winner of the *Overland* Judith Wright Poetry Prize. Her work has appeared in journals such as *Cordite, Blackbox Manifold, Overland* and *Westerly.* She is the author of *Greatest Hit* (Vagabond Press) and the chapbooks *Hip Shifts* (If A Leaf Falls Press) and *Deluxe Paperweight* (Stale Objects dePress).

Andy Jackson is a poet, creative writing teacher and mentor, and a Patron of Writers Victoria. He was the inaugural Writing the Future of Health Fellow, and has co-edited disability-themed issues of *Southerly* and *Australian Poetry Journal.* Andy's latest poetry collection is *Human Looking,* which won the ALS Gold Medal and the Prime Minister's Literary Award for Poetry.

Ella Jeffery is a poet, editor and critic. Her debut collection of poems, *Dead Bolt,* won the Puncher & Wattmann Prize for a First Book of Poems, the Anne Elder Award, and was shortlisted for the Dame Mary Gilmore Award. Her poetry has appeared widely in journals and anthologies including *Best Australian Poems, Meanjin, HEAT, Griffith Review* and *Island.* She is the recipient of a Queensland Writers Fellowship, the Mick Dark Fellowship for Environmental Writing, and the Queensland Premier's Young Publishers and Writers Award. She lives in Brisbane.

Hannah Jenkins is an arts writer and poet specialising in digital works and online writing experiments. They are the Co-Founder & Co-Editor of *Crawlspace,* a digital platform publishing interactive and multimedia writing and art that experiments with the expansive freedom the web offers. Hannah's poetry has been shortlisted for the Woollahra Digital Literary Award in both 2021 and 2022. You can find their work in *Cordite, Taper, Overland, Running Dog, Runway, The Suburban Review, Scum Mag* and more.

A. Frances Johnson is an award-winning writer and artist with creative research and teaching interests in postcolonialism, ecocritical art and ecopoetics. Amanda has published four collections of poetry, a novel and a monograph. Awards include the Griffith University Josephine Ulrick Poetry Prize (2016), the international *ABR* Peter Porter Poetry Prize (2020) and Wesley Michel Wright Prize (2012). Two recent solo exhibitions *Sunset Clause* (2021) and *Colonial Heat* (2021) counterpoint environmental themes explored in her recent poetry collection *Save As* (2022).

Jill Jones lives on unceded Kaurna land. Her latest book is *Acrobat Music: New and Selected Poems.* Other recent books include *Wild Curious Air*—winner of the 2021 Wesley Michel Wright Prize, *A History Of What I'll Become*—shortlisted for the 2021 Kenneth Slessor Award and the 2022 John Bray Award, and *Viva the Real*—shortlisted for the 2019 Prime Minister's Literary Award for Poetry. Her work is widely published in Australia, Canada, Ireland, NZ, Singapore, Sweden, UK and USA. She writes and teaches freelance, and previously worked as an academic, arts administrator, journalist and book editor.

Lesh Karan is a Naarm/Melbourne-based poet and essayist. Her publications include *Australian Poetry, Best of Australian Poems 2022, Cordite, Island, Mascara, Overland, Rabbit* and *Red Room Poetry,* amongst others. In 2023, she won the Liquid Amber Poetry Prize and was shortlisted for the *Overland* Judith Wright Poetry Prize. Lesh is of Fiji Indian background, and shares a house with her hubby and fur baby.

S. K. Kelen has been composing poems since before the Trojan War. His most recent books are *A Happening in Hades* (Puncher & Wattmann, 2020), and *Love's Philosophy* (Life Before Man/Gazebo Books, 2020).

John Kinsella is the author of over forty books. His many awards include the Australian Prime Minister's Literary Award for Poetry, the Victorian Premier's Award for Poetry, the John Bray Poetry Award, the Judith Wright Calanthe Award for Poetry and the Western Australian Premier's Award for Poetry (three times). His latest books are *Lucida Intervalla* and *The Collected Poems of Christopher Brennan* (UWA Publishing, 2018 and 2019); *On the Outskirts* (UQP, 2017), and *Drowning in Wheat: Selected Poems* (Picador, 2016). He is a a Fellow of Churchill College, Cambridge University, and Professor of Literature and Environment at Curtin University, Western Australia. He lives on Ballardong Noongar land at Jam Tree Gully in the Western Australian wheatbelt. In 2007 he received the Christopher Brennan Award for Lifetime Achievement in Poetry.

Yeena Kirkbright is a Wiradjuri poet, now based on Dharug and Gadigal lands in Sydney. She has been a participant in Sweatshop's All About Women of Colour emerging writers mentorship program, a runner-up in the Kuracca Prize for Australian Literature and awarded second place in the 2022 *Overland* Judith Wright Poetry Prize. Her work has appeared in several literary journals and anthologies.

Abbra Kotlarczyk was raised on Bundjalung Country in the subtropical ruins of a decommissioned banana plantation. She makes art, curates, reads, writes, edits, parents and gardens (sometimes all at once) in an attempt to outmanoeuvre the forces that pit us against enmeshment. Recent writing has appeared in *Australian Poetry Journal* 12.2: suite, sequence, *Tell Me Like You Mean It* Vol. 6, *Best of Australian Poems 2021, Overland, No More Poetry, Cordite Poetry Review, un Magazine, Minarets* and elsewhere. A poem of hers won the *Overland* Judith Wright Poetry Prize in 2022.

Jo Langdon is the author of two poetry collections: a chapbook, *Snowline* (Whitmore Press, 2012) and *Glass Life* (Five Islands Press, 2018). Her recent fiction and poetry also appear in journals including *Cordite Poetry Review, Griffith Review, Island, Overland, Rabbit* and *Westerly*. Jo lives on unceded Wadawurrung land in Geelong, Victoria.

Tyberius Larking is a 20-year-old Mirning and South Asian poet and illustrator of trans experience practicing on Kaurna land. In his writing, native organisms and their eco-issues always make an appearance, as insignia of his personal and culturally inspired commitment to their preservation and respect for their tenacious persistence, their unique generosity and cooperative equilibrium. Still, his poetry is less artisanal or orderly, and more earnest and instinctive.

Jeanine Leane is an activist, poet, writer and teacher who belongs to the Wiradjuri people of the Murrumbidgee River near Gundagai. Jeanine currently lives and work on the lands of the East Kulin Nations of Naarm Melbourne.

Neika Lehman is a writer from nipaluna | Hobart who resides in Narrm | Melbourne. Their poetry, essays and criticism appear in *un Mag, Art + Australia, The Saturday Paper, Cordite, Overland, Australian Poetry Journal* and *The Suburban Review* among others.

Kate Lilley is the author of three books of poetry—most recently *Tilt* (Vagabond, 2018), winner of the Victorian Premier's Award for Poetry—and many essays. She has edited two collections, *Margaret Cavendish: The Blazing World and Other Writings* (Penguin Classics) and *Dorothy Hewett: Selected Poems* (UWAP). She was a member of the English Department at the University of Sydney 1990–2021 where she is now an Honorary Associate Professor.

Rozanna Lilley is a poet and essayist. Her poems are widely published in literary journals and anthologised in various collections, including *Best Australian Poems* (Black Inc, 2015) and *Admissions* (Upswell, 2022). Her hybrid prose-poetry memoir *Do Oysters Get Bored? A Curious Life* (UWA Publishing, 2018) was shortlisted for the National Biography Award in 2019. In 2022, Rozanna was shortlisted for the Red Room Poetry Fellowship. Her first stand-alone poetry collection, *The Lady in the Bottle* (Eyewear Publishing), which revisits the 1960s TV series *I Dream of Jeannie,* was published in 2023. More details can be found at: rozannalilley.com.au.

Jennifer Maiden has published twenty-eight poetry collections, six novels and three nonfiction works. Awards include three Kenneth Slessor Prizes, two CJ Dennis Prizes, Victorian Prize for Literature, Christopher Brennan Award, two Age Poetry Book of Year, Age Book of Year, ALS Gold Medal. Her *Liquid Nitrogen* was shortlisted Griffin International Prize. Her latest books, published by Quemar Press: poetry collections *Selected Poems 1967–2018, Appalachian Fall, brookings: the noun, The Espionage Act, Biological Necessity, Ox in Metal, Golden Bridge*; workbook *Workbook Questions: Writing of Torture, Trauma*; five *Play With Knives* novels; booklength essays *The Cuckold and the Vampires, The Laps of the Gods.*

Philip Mead was inaugural Chair of Australian Literature at the University of Western Australia (2009–2018). He is currently Emeritus Professor, University of Western Australia, and Honorary Professorial Fellow in the Melbourne Graduate School of Education, University of Melbourne. In 2018 Philip published *Antipodal Shakespeare: Remembering and Forgetting in Britain, Australia and New Zealand, 1916–2016* (with Gordon McMullan, Bloomsbury); *The Social Work of Narrative: human rights and the cultural imaginary* (ed. with Gareth Griffiths, Columbia University Press); and *The Literature of Tasmania* (AustLit Resource).

Ari Mills is a proud Kuku Yalanji and Nangu writer and poet. Ari centres their writing in Indigenous and LGBTQI+ communities through expressions of love and decolonial praxis in storytelling. Ari's first writing publication appearance was at the start of 2023 with BLACKBOOKS in their anthology titled *NANGAMAY MANA DJURALI dream gather grow.*

Scott-Patrick Mitchell is the author of *Clean,* a poetry collection which explores their lived experience with addiction and recovery. *Clean* was shortlisted for the Victorian Premier's Literary Awards for Poetry, the 2023 Western Australian Premier's Book Awards Book of The Year Category and named in *Australian Book Review*'s list of Books of 2022. Mitchell was the 2022 Red Room Poetry Fellow.

Sam Moginie's recent poetry publications include *Heel on Desk* (now orries, 2023) and *Let's Shake On It?* (S0d Books, 2022). With Eddie Hopely, Sam has produced *Forest Ladder 1* (2020) and *(Web 1) Sensu/Go Saga I: Mascle Concealer* (2022), and three albums which appear under Gooey Frog Kite, most recently *Puppy Pastry As Vexing Dog Guard.* Album *Earth Bully* by Mrs Sam also appeared in 2023.

Jazz Money is a Wiradjuri poet and artist based on Gadigal land, Sydney. Her practice is centred around poetics while producing works that encompass installation, digital, performance, film and print. Jazz's writing and art has been widely presented, performed and published nationally and internationally. Their first poetry collection, the best-selling *how to make a basket* (UQP, 2021), won the David Unaipon Award.

Gareth Morgan is the author of *When A Punk Becomes A Spunk* and *Dear Eileen*, and co-director of Sick Leave.

Leah Muddle is an artist, poet and retail worker. In 2023, she made new work for *Sick Leave, Australian Poetry Journal* 12.2, and for the exhibition *Renee So: Provenance* at Monash University Museum of Art.

π.O. is a legendary figure in the Australian poetry scene, the chronicler of Melbourne and its culture and migrations, and a highly disciplined anarchist. He is the publisher of *Unusual Work* by Collective Effort Press, a long-time magazine editor, a pioneer of performance poetry in Australia, and the author of many collections—including *Heide*, which was shortlisted for the Prime Minister's Literary Award for Poetry and received the Judith Wright Calanthe Award. His latest work, *The Tour*, was published by Giramondo in 2023.

Ella O'Keefe is a poet and researcher who lives in Melbourne, on unceded Wurundjeri land. Her previous publications include *Slowlier* (2021) and *Rhinestone* (2015).

Esther Ottaway's poems have been shortlisted in the international poetry prizes, the Montreal, Bridport, MPU International and Mslexia, and she has won the Tim Thorne Prize for Poetry, the Tom Collins Poetry Prize, the Queensland Poetry Festival Ekphrasis Award and other prizes. Her acclaimed new collection, *She Doesn't Seem Autistic* (Puncher & Wattmann), creatively illuminates the hidden experiences of women and girls on the autism spectrum. She co-edited, with Scott-Patrick Mitchell, *Australian Poetry Journal* 12.1: divergence, relevance, and is co-editing, with Andy Jackson and Kerri Shying, *Raging Grace: Australian writers speak out on disability* (Puncher & Wattmann).

Luke Patterson is a Gamilaroi poet, folklorist and musician living on Gadigal lands. His poetry has appeared in *Cordite, Plumwood Mountain, Rabbit, Running Dog* and *The Suburban Review.* He has also featured in the anthologies *Active Aesthetics, Firefront: First Nation's poetry and power today* and *Best of Australian Poems 2021*. His research and creative pursuits are grounded in extensive work with First Nations and other community-based organisations across Australia.

Sarah Pearce is a poet, editor and researcher from Tarndanya (Adelaide). Her work appears in *Meniscus, Writing from Below, TEXT, The Suburban Review, Overland, Cordite* and various anthologies. She has held residencies at Adelaide City Library, FELTspace gallery and Gunyah, and performed at Blenheim and Adelaide Fringe Festivals. She writes about embodiment, the Gothic, queer narratives and mental health.

D. Perez-McVie is a poet and a clerk. Their chapbook *Gender Is the Extent We Go To in Order To Be Loved* is forthcoming as part of the Slow Loris series from Puncher & Wattmann. They live on Wurundjeri country.

Anupama Pilbrow is the Reviews Editor at *Cordite Poetry Review.* She is a PhD candidate at the University of New South Wales researching early utopian fiction and representations of water. She is the author of chapbook *Body Poems,* released as part of the deciBels 3 series (Vagabond, 2018).

Vidya Rajan is a multi-disciplinary artist often working across screenwriting, theatre, comedy and digital space.

Andrea Rassell is a media artist and interdisciplinary researcher in science art. Working in nanoart—artforms that engage with nanoscience and nanotechnology—she creates experimental films and moving image installations that explore our perception of the nanoscale realm. She is a creative research fellow at the Curtin HIVE (Hub for Immersive Visualisation and eResearch).

Harry Reid is a poet & co-director of Sick Leave. Harry is the author of *Leave Me Alone* (Cordite Books, 2022) & *the best way to destroy an enemy is to make him a friend* (Puncher & Wattmann, 2020).

Peter Rose is the author of six poetry collections, two novels and a family memoir. His series The Catullan Rag—satires and elegies in the style of the Roman poet Catullus—began in 1990. His newest book of poems is *Rag* (Gazebo Books, 2023).

Autumn Royal creates drama, poetry and criticism.

Brendan Ryan lives in Australia. The author of six collections of poetry, his memoir, *Walk Like a Cow,* was published in 2020 by Walleah Press. A new collection of poetry, *Feldspar,* will be published by Recent Work Press in 2023.

Omar Sakr is a poet and writer born in Western Sydney to Lebanese and Turkish migrants. He is the acclaimed author of the novel *Son of Sin* (Affirm Press, 2022) and three poetry collections, notably *The Lost Arabs* (University of Queensland Press, 2019), which won the 2020 Prime Minister's Literary Award. He was the first Arab-Australian Muslim to win this prestigious award. Omar's poems have been published in English, Arabic and Spanish, featuring in *POETRY Magazine,* Poets.org *Poem-a-Day, Poetry London, Prairie Schooner, Hazlitt, Mizna, Overland, Australian Book Review* and *Griffith Review,* among others. His new book is *Non-Essential Work* (UQP, 2023).

Alex Skovron is the author of seven collections of poetry, a prose novella and a book of short stories. His most recent collection of poems is *Letters from the Periphery* (2021); his earlier volume of new and selected poems, *Towards the Equator* (2014), was shortlisted in the Prime Minister's Literary Awards. His work has been translated into a number of languages, including French, Czech, Chinese, Dutch and Polish. He is currently preparing a new collection in prose and verse.

Alicia Sometimes is an Australian poet and broadcaster. She has performed her spoken word and poetry at many venues, festivals and events around the world. Her poems have been published in *Best Australian Science Writing, Best Australian Poems, The Age, Griffith Review, Meanjin, Westerly* and more. In 2021 she completed the Boyd Garret residency for the City of Melbourne and a Virtual Writer in Residency for Manchester City of Literature and Manchester Literature Festival. In 2023 she has received ANAT's Synapse Artist Residency and has co-created an art installation for Science Gallery Melbourne's upcoming exhibition, *Dark Matters.*

Pete Spence was born in 1946. He is a poet, visual poet, editor and filmmaker, and has worked in various jobs to cover the ongoing deficit. A collection of his visual poetry, *5 X Y*, was published last year by Red Fox Press as part of the C'est Mon Dada series.

Andrew Sutherland (he/they) is a Queer Poz (PLHIV) writer and performance-maker between Boorloo (Perth) and Singapore. His work draws upon Queer and intercultural ways of being, filtering autobiographical practices through the lens of pop-cultural, ecological and viral dramaturgies. Andrew's debut poetry collection *Paradise (point of transmission)* was published by Fremantle Press in 2022, and his poetry, fiction and creative non-fiction can be found in a range of publications, including *Westerly, Island, Overland, Portside Review, Australian Poetry Journal, Running Dog, EXHALE: an anthology of Queer voices from Singapore, Best of Australian Poems 2021,* among others. Andrew is grateful to reside on unceded Whadjuk Noongar land.

Josie/Jocelyn Suzanne is a freelance editor/writer/programmer. Their work has appeared in *Cordite, Rabbit Journal* and *Overland,* among others. They were shortlisted for the 2022 Val Vallis Award, and were the recipient of the 2021 Harri Jones Memorial Prize for Poetry, as well as being one of the 2021 Next Chapter recipients. They are a genderqueer trans femme and live on unceded Wurundjeri land in Naarm.

Thabani Tshuma is a Zimbabwean writer and performance poet based in Naarm. His work can be found in publications such as *Dichotomi, Next in Colour, CUBBY ART, Cordite Poetry Review* and ABC ArtWorks's *SLAMMED.* Thabani is co-curator of Thin Red Lines, and his debut collection *The Gospel of Unmade Creation* was released in 2023 through Recent Work Press.

Saaro Umar is a writer.

Lucy Van writes poetry and criticism. Her collection, *The Open* (Cordite Books, 2021), was longlisted for the Stella Prize, shortlisted for the Mary Gilmore Award and highly commended in the Anne Elder Award. She teaches poetry at the University of Melbourne.

Siân Vate has published the chapbooks *feels right* (Slow Loris) and *end motion / manifest* (Bulky News). Her work has appeared with *otoliths, E·ratio* (NYC), *Cordite* and *artiCHOKE* (Berlin). She lives between Melbourne and regional NSW.

Catherine Vidler grew up in Newcastle, studied in Sydney, and then lived and worked in the US and New Zealand for several years before returning to Sydney in 2004. Her poetry has been widely published in Australia, New Zealand, the US, the UK and elsewhere.

Dženana Vucic is a Bosnian-Australian writer, poet and critic. She has received the 2022 Marten Bequest, the 2022 Peter Blazey Fellowship, and the 2021 Kat Muscat Fellowship to work on a book about the Bosnian war, identity, memory and un/belonging. In 2023 she was a *Kill Your Darlings* New Critic. Her writing has appeared widely in so-called Australia and overseas.

Corey Wakeling is a writer, scholar and translator living in Tokyo. He is the author of three collections, and *Debts of the Robots*, his fourth, will be published in 2024 by Cordite Books. Receiving a PhD in English from the University of Melbourne in 2013, Corey is active as a scholar of modern and contemporary literature and performance. His first monograph is *Beckett's Laboratory* (Bloomsbury, 2021), his second is *Situation, Inertia, and Inconvenience in Japanese Contemporary Performance* (Routledge, forthcoming). He is Associate Professor of English literature in the College of Education, Psychology and Human Studies at Aoyama Gakuin University.

Petra White lives in Belfast. Her most recent collection is *Cities* (Vagabond Press, 2021).

Jessica L. Wilkinson has published three poetic biographies, *Marionette: A Biography of Miss Marion Davies* (Vagabond, 2012), *Suite for Percy Grainger* (Vagabond, 2014) and *Music Made Visible: A Biography of George Balanchine* (Vagabond, 2019). She is the founding editor of *Rabbit: a journal for nonfiction poetry* and the offshoot Rabbit Poets Series of single-author collections by emerging Australian poets. She co-edited the anthologies *Contemporary Australian Feminist Poetry* (2016) and *Memory Book: Portraits of Older Australians in Poetry and Watercolours* (2021). She is an associate professor in creative writing at RMIT University, Melbourne.

Tim Wright is the author of *Suns* and *The night's live changes.*

Ouyang Yu has published 148 books of poetry, fiction, non-fiction, literary translation and criticism in English and Chinese languages, including his award-winning novels—*The Eastern Slope Chronicle* (2002) and *The English Class* (2010), his collections of poetry—*Songs of the Last Chinese Poet* (1997) and *Terminally Poetic* (2020), which won the Judith Wright Calanthe Award for Poetry in the 2021 Queensland Literary Awards. He was shortlisted for the Writer's Prize in the 2021 Melbourne Prize for Literature and won the Fellowship from the Australia Council in late 2021 for writing a documentary novel.

Gavin Yuan Gao is a Meanjin-based poet and translator. Their debut poetry collection, *At the Altar of Touch*, was released by the University of Queensland Press in 2022 and won the 2023 Victorian Premier's Prize for Poetry. They are currently a James A. Michener Fellow at the Michener Center for Writers.

Guest Editors

Gig Ryan's *New and Selected Poems* (Giramondo, 2011); *Selected Poems*, (Bloodaxe Books, U.K.), was winner of the 2012 Grace Leven Prize for Poetry and the 2012 Kenneth Slessor Prize for Poetry. She has also written songs with Disband on *Six Goodbyes* (1988), and with Driving Past on *Real Estate* (1999) and *Travel* (2006). She was Poetry Editor of *The Age* from 1998–2016. She is a freelance reviewer; next book forthcoming eventually.

Panda Wong is a Malaysian-Chinese poet who lives on unceded Wurundjeri land. Her first chapbook *angel wings dumpster fire* was published by Puncher & Wattmann in 2022. Her first EP *salmon cannon me into the abyss*, a collaboration with multiple friends, was released in July 2022. She was also shortlisted for the *Overland* Judith Wright Poetry Prize 2022.

Acknowledgements and Publication Details

Jordie Albiston's 'a night' first appeared on page 90 of her posthumously published collection *Frank*, National Library of Australia Publishing, May 2023.

Susie Anderson's 'sidney nolan' first appeared in her collection *the body country*, Hachette, July 2023.

Louis Armand's 'DI/ODE CLXX' first appeared in *Overland* 250, June 2023. It was subsequently featured in Armand's collection *DI/ODE I–CCCX*, International Arts Centre Prague, August 2023.

Alison J Barton's 'as we are' first appeared in *Cordite* 108: Dedication, February 2023.

Ender Başkan's 'a workers paradise' first appeared in *Unusual Work* 35, Collective Effort Press, May 2023.

Luke Beesley's 'Death in the Family' first appeared in *In the Photograph*, Giramondo, July 2023.

Judith Beveridge's 'Bluebottles' first appeared in *HEAT* Series 3, Number 8, April 2023.

Javant Biarujia's '"CAVAFY"' first appeared in *otoliths* 69, May 2023.

Eva Birch's 'Bourne Again' first appeared in *Sick Leave Party Reports* Round 1, February 2023.

Ken Bolton's 'MIDWINTER DAY' first appeared in *otoliths* 69, May 2023.

Andrew Brooks and **Arvind Rosa Brooks**'s 'Year of the Ox' first appeared in *Liminal* Mirror, October 2022.

Pam Brown's 'Pulp to reform' was selected from the *Best of Australian Poems 2023* open callout and at this time was unpublished. It was later published in *Cordite* 110: POP!, September 2023.

Melinda Bufton's 'Heatless curls' first appeared in *Sick Leave Party Reports* Round 1, February 2023.

joanne burns's 'two rat poems' first appeared in *Overland*'s Friday Poetry series, March 2023.

Broede Carmody's excerpt from *Shouldering Pine* first appeared on pages 47–50 of his book-length work *Shouldering Pine*, Vagabond Press, February 2023.

Eileen Chong's 'Dirge' was published in *Going Down Swinging* The Funeral, October 2022.

Justin Clemens's 'the problem of evil' was commissioned by Pascalle Burton for a session dedicated to the work of David Lynch at Queensland Poetry Festival, 2015. It was first published in the collection *A Foul Wind*, Hunter Publishers Australia, January 2023.

Ali Cobby Eckermann's excerpt from *She is the Earth* first appeared on pages 8–9 of her book length work *She is the Earth*, Magabala Books, May 2023.

Alex Creece's 'i ain't reading all that / i'm happy for you tho / or sorry that happened' was selected from the *Best of Australian Poems 2023* open callout and at this time was unpublished. It was later published in *Cordite* 110: POP!, September 2023.

Amy Crutchfield's 'Wasp' first appeared in *Island* 168, July 2023.

Madeleine Dale's 'Crush Fracture' first appeared in her chapbook *On Fire with Dangerous Cargo*, Queensland Poetry, April 2023.

Shastra Deo's 'Nothing Nowhere At Some Point' was published by Red Room Poetry, January 2023. It subsequently appeared in *A Line in the Sand: 20 Years of Red Room Poetry*, Pantera Press, August 2023.

Elese Dowden's 'chronic swooners production era' was a previously unpublished poem selected from the *Best of Australian Poems 2023* open callout.

Dave Drayton's 'the cost price of a flaming gala' was a finalist for the 2022 Newcastle Poetry Prize, and subsequently published in *The Anabranch: Newcastle Poetry Prize 2022*, Hunter Writers Centre, September 2022.

Laurie Duggan's 'What me worry' is a previously unpublished poem selected from the *Best of Australian Poems 2023* open callout.

Theodore Ell's 'Heyday' first appeared in his collection *Beginning in Sight*, Recent Work Press, July 2022.

Michael Farrell's 'Barks of Great Artists' first appeared in *Meanjin* 82.1, March 2023.

Liam Ferney's 'License to Drive' first appeared in *Overland* 249, March 2023.

Toby Fitch's 'Elegy for a Staffy' is a previously unpublished poem selected from the *Best of Australian Poems 2023* open callout. It is forthcoming for publication in the *Weekend Australian*.

Joan Fleming's 'Coins, Glass, Nails, Pottery, Cinders' first appeared in *ABR* May 2023.

Zenobia Frost's 'For Exodus' was shortlisted for the 2023 Gwen Harwood Poetry Prize, and subsequently appeared in *Island* 167, March 2023.

Lou Garcia-Dolnik's 'citations for a dream' first appeared in *un Magazine* 16.2, A Collection of Annotated Bibliographies Vol. 2, November 2022.

Angela Gardner's 'Due Point' is a previously unpublished poem selected from the *Best of Australian Poems 2023* open callout.

Kathryn Gledhill-Tucker's 'general instructions for operating' first appeared in *Running Dog*, August 2022.

Madison Godfrey's 'Crystalline' first appeared in their collection *Dress Rehearsals*, JOAN, February 2023.

Jake Goetz's 'A Message From the NRMA' first appeared in *Overland* 247, October 2022.

Lisa Gorton's 'The Pazzi Conspiracy Medal' first appeared in her collection *Mirabilia,* Giramondo, August 2022.

Rory Green's 'Catalogue of Deaths' is a previously unpublished poem selected from the *Best of Australian Poems 2023* open callout.

Natalie Harkin's 'impossible to contain' first appeared in *NANGAMAY MANA DJURALI dream gather grow — First Nations Australia LGBTQIA+ Poetry,* BLACKBOOKS, February 2023.

John Hawke's 'Circle of Fifths' first appeared in *ABR* November 2022.

Kris Hemensley's 'Topography' first appeared within a collection of three elegies published in *Cordite* 106: Open, September 2022.

Fiona Hile's 'Wheatmania' first appeared in *APJ* 12.2: suite, sequence, June 2023.

Dan Hogan's 'Blade of Grass, Meadow of Knives' was first published under the title 'What fangs out of the bracken with a head full of garden?' by Red Room Poetry, August 2022. It subsequently appeared under its current title in Hogan's collection *Secret Third Thing,* Cordite Books, May 2023.

LK Holt's 'The Smiles' is a previously unpublished poem selected from the *Best of Australian Poems 2023* open callout.

Duncan Hose's 'Ringaskiddy Oratory' first appeared in *NO PLACEBOS* 5, Donnithorne Street Press, May 2023.

Hasib Hourani's 'winter jumper' first appeared in *Going Down Swinging,* July 2023.

Holly Isemonger's 'Genesis: I: I-VIII' first appeared in *Social Alternatives* Focus on Fiction vol. 41 no. 3, November 2022. It subsequently appeared in Isemonger's collection *Greatest Hit,* Vagabond Press, February 2023.

Ella Jeffery's 'Homebody' first appeared in *HEAT* Series 3 Number 4, August 2022.

Hannah Jenkins's 'Island Layer' first appeared in *The Suburban Review,* March 2023.

A. Frances Johnson's 'Caravaggio in Rome' is a previously unpublished poem selected from the *Best of Australian Poems 2023* open callout.

Jill Jones's 'Little Heartbeats' first appeared in her collection *Acrobat Music: New & Selected Poems,* Puncher & Wattmann, June 2023.

Lesh Karan's 'tinnitus as hushing haibun' was shortlisted for the 2022 *Overland* Judith Wright Poetry Prize, and subsequently appeared in *Overland* 250, June 2023.

S. K. Kelen's 'Reality' first appeared in *otoliths* 70, 1 August 2023.

John Kinsella's 'Incognito' first appeared in *Poetry Magazine*, June 2023.

Yeena Kirkbright's 'Camperdown Grief Junk' received second place in the 2022 *Overland* Judith Wright Poetry Prize, and subsequently appeared in *Overland* 250, June 2023.

Abbra Kotlarczyk's 'My Kathy Acker' first appeared in *Tell Me Like You Mean It* Vol. 6, *Cordite* x Australian Poetry, June 2023.

Jo Langdon's 'Windscreen' first appeared in *Plumwood Mountain* Vol. 9 No. 1, September 2022.

Tyberius Larking's 'Let Everyone Touch Red Dirt' first appeared in *Voiceworks* Static, May 2023.

Jeanine Leane's 'Biladurang untranslated' is a previously unpublished poem selected from the *Best of Australian Poems 2023* open callout. It is set to be published in Leane's 2024 collection with University of Queensland Press.

Neika Lehman's 'Sea Glass' first appeared (with slight textual differences) in *NANGAMAY MANA DJURALI dream gather grow — First Nations Australia LGBTQIA+ Poetry*, BLACKBOOKS, February 2023.

Kate Lilley's 'Hic Mulier' first appeared in *APJ* 12.2: suite, sequence, June 2023.

Rozanna Lilley's '*El Dorado* (after) life' first appeared in *Westerly* 67.2, November 2022.

Jennifer Maiden's 'Gore Vidal Woke Up on Julian Assange's 52nd Birthday' first appeared on Quemar Press's website, June 2023. It will feature in her forthcoming collection with Quemar Press, *The China Shelf*.

Philip Mead's 'Déjà Rêvé' first appeared in *ABR* April 2023.

Ari Mills's 'Personless Love' first appeared in *NANGAMAY MANA DJURALI dream gather grow — First Nations Australia LGBTQIA+ Poetry*, BLACKBOOKS, February 2023.

Scott-Patrick Mitchell's 'A Lullaby Made From Ice' first appeared in *Griffith Review* 77: Real Cool World, August 2022.

Sam Moginie's 'Crisis Let Me Vase' first appeared in their chapbook *Heel on Desk*, now orries press, April 2023.

Jazz Money's 'post glitch' first appeared in *Crawlspace* Issue 1, November 2022.

Gareth Morgan's 'Prospect Park' first appeared in *HEAT* Series 3 Number 7, February 2023.

Leah Muddle's 'why not' is a previously unpublished poem selected from the *Best of Australian Poems 2023* open callout.

π.O.'s 'Boarding House' first appeared in *HEAT* Series 3 Number 7, February 2023.

Ella O'Keefe's 'swathes of it' is a previously unpublished poem selected from the *Best of Australian Poems 2023* open callout. It is set to be published in O'Keefe's forthcoming chapbook *the year in water*, Slow Loris.

Esther Ottaway's 'After writing a book on female autism, I decide to bury it' and **Andy Jackson**'s 'After reading her poem, I remember the diagnosis they give me' first appeared in *Island* 166, November 2022.

Luke Patterson's 'A Grass Tree by Any Other Name' first appeared in *NANGAMAY MANA DJURALI dream gather grow — First Nations Australia LGBTQIA+ Poetry*, BLACKBOOKS, February 2023.

Sarah Pearce's 'Wednesday at Gunyah' first appeared in *Overland* 248, December 2022.

D. Perez-McVie's 'Blue' is a previously unpublished poem selected from the *Best of Australian Poems 2023* open callout. It is set to be published in Perez-McVie's forthcoming chapbook with Slow Loris.

Anupama Pilbrow's 'Excerpt from [redacted] Poem' first appeared in *Liminal* Here: Eros & the Like, 1 August 2023.

Vidya Rajan's 'Untitled Wild Geese Game' first appeared in the *Liminal* and *Cordite* collaboration *Cordite* 107: Cordite x Liminal, December 2022.

Harry Reid's 'restore previous tabs' first appeared in the collection *Leave Me Alone*, Cordite Books, August 2022.

Peter Rose's 'Two Thousand and One Nights' first appeared in *Meanjin* 82.1, March 2023.

Autumn Royal's 'Poesy' first appeared in *Cordite* 106: Open, September 2022.

Brendan Ryan's 'Taking it Slow' first appeared in *Westerly* 68.1, July 2023. It was subsequently featured in Ryan's collection *Felspar*, Recent Work Press, September 2023.

Omar Sakr's poem, 'Relevant to the Day' appeared in a previous form in *Stillpoint*, April 2020. This version was featured in his collection *Non-Essential Work*, University of Queensland Press, April 2023.

Alex Skovron's 'The Hourglass and the Pledge' first appeared in *Live Encounters Poetry & Writing*, December 2022.

Alicia Sometimes's 'Bose-Einstein Condensate' first appeared in *Baby Teeth Journal*, April 2023, with sound from **Andrea Rassell**.

Pete Spence's 'No Picnic!' first appeared in *otoliths* 66, August 2022.

Andrew Sutherland's 'Gorgon' appeared in a previous form in *Crab Fat Magazine*. This version was featured in their collection *Paradise (point of transmission)*, Fremantle Press, August 2022.

Josie/Jocelyn Suzanne's 'The Resurrection of the Body as Zombie Movie' first appeared in *#Enbylife*, May 2023.

Thabani Tshuma's 'Sixth Sense' first appeared on ABC Arts's *Slammed*, May 2023. It was subsequently included in his collection *The Gospel of Unmade Creation*, Recent Work Press, September 2023.

Saaro Umar's 'weaverbird' was commissioned and published for Renee So's Solo exhibition, *Provenance*, which opened May 2023 at MUMA. It was written in response to the work, 'Venus of Valdivia', 2019.

Lucy Van's 'Verrition' first appeared in the *Liminal* and *Cordite* collaboration *Cordite* 107: Cordite x Liminal, December 2022.

Siân Vate's 'things that heat' first appeared in *APJ* 12.2: suite, sequence, June 2023.

Catherine Vidler's 'foils of cloud' first appeared in *Blackbox Manifold* issue 30, July 2023.

Dženana Vucic's 'To Learn a M/other Tongue' first appeared in *Australian Multilingual Writing Project* Issue 6, October 2022.

Corey Wakeling's 'The Sound of Hammering' is a previously unpublished poem selected from the *Best of Australian Poems 2023* open callout.

Petra White's 'Passing Through Chicago' first appeared in *PN Review* 269, Vol. 49 No. 3, January 2023.

Jessica L. Wilkinson's 'Scissors and Clamps' appeared in *Meanjin* 81.3, September 2023.

Tim Wright's 'February' first appeared in *otoliths* 69, May 2023.

Ouyang Yu's 'My TED Talk:' first appeared in *Overland*'s Friday Poetry series, May 2023.

Gavin Yuan Gao's 'Ghost Money' first appeared in *Hayden's Ferry Review* 71, January 2023.

www.ingramcontent.com/pod-product-compliance
Lightning Source LLC
Chambersburg PA
CBHW021148160426
43194CB00007B/737
* 9 7 8 0 9 9 2 3 1 8 9 4 9 *